CHILDREN OF THE ATOMIC BOMB

Asia-Pacific: Culture, Politics, and Society

Editors: Rey Chow, Arif Dirlik,

H. D. Harootunian, and Masao Miyoshi

CHILDREN OF THE ATOMIC BOMB

An American Physician's Memoir of Nagasaki,

Hiroshima, and the Marshall Islands

JAMES N. YAMAZAKI with Louis B. Fleming

DUKE UNIVERSITY PRESS   *Durham and London 1995*

The costs of publication for this book have been supported in
part by a 1994 Hiromi Arisawa Award, given to Duke University
Press for publication of an outstanding work on Japan.
© 1995 Duke University Press   All rights reserved
Printed in the United States of America on acid-free paper ∞
Typeset in Berthold Bodoni Antiqua by Tseng Information Systems, Inc.
Library of Congress Cataloging-in-Publication Data appear
on the last printed page of this book.

CONTENTS

FOREWORD
John W. Dower

When Dr. James Yamazaki visited Japan in 1989, he attended a meeting of mothers in Hiroshima who were parents of "pica babies." *Pica* is a familiar euphemism to most Japanese, referring to the blinding flash of the atomic bomb and conveying a vivid sense of thermal burns and radiation poisoning. The "pica babies" were children born with abnormalities, including mental retardation, after being exposed to radiation in the womb when the bombs were dropped on Hiroshima and Nagasaki. They were forty-four years old in 1989.

Dr. Yamazaki marveled at the quiet way the now elderly mothers of these retarded child-adults told their stories, and he grieved over the uncertainty that haunted them concerning what would become of these children of the atomic bomb when they, the parents, died. We, in turn, can only be impressed by the quiet way he himself tells his own remarkable personal story, in which this is but a part.

This is a story of striking juxtapositions—a snapshot of an American life, as it were, that captures in a single frame racial prejudice in the United States, the horror of the war in Europe, and the human impact of the atomic bomb. And yet we read this brief personal account, chapter after terse chapter, with a persistent sense of how decent and constructive the human spirit can be. James Yamazaki, pediatrician and medical researcher, made an early commitment to making children whole. Son of an Episcopal priest, his own vision has been consistently humanistic, his moral sense as solid as a rock.

There are compelling subthemes here, captivating vignettes. Like thousands of other second-generation Japanese-Americans, Dr. Yamazaki fought for his country while his parents were incarcerated behind barbed wire in one of the now notorious U.S. internment camps. Captured by the Germans in the Battle of the Bulge, he too experienced prison camps, as well as bombardment by U.S. aircraft, not once but twice. Sent to occupied Japan in 1949 to study the effects of nuclear radiation on children, he and his family were discriminated against by the British Commonwealth forces occupying Hiroshima, whose military facilities and social events were reserved for persons "of European descent only." His experience of the disparity between professed democratic ideals and actual practice only strengthened his embrace of the ideals.

Subsequently posted to Nagasaki, apparently as a kind of exile for protesting such racist policies in Hiroshima, Dr. Yamazaki embarked on research concerning the medical effects of the atomic bomb without ever being informed of the existence of earlier U.S. scientific reports on this subject. Such obsessive secrecy was standard practice and had ramifications that extended beyond the scope of the present account. The policy that led the U.S. government to keep even its own qualified researchers from knowing about prior studies also kept important information about the human effects of the bombs out of the hands of Japanese doctors laboring to tend to the victims. It was not until 1951, near the end of the postwar Allied occupation of Japan, that Japanese researchers were even permitted to present papers on the medical consequences of the bombs. Decoding the full significance of Hiroshima and Nagasaki has been an ongoing struggle ever since August 1945.

Today, a half century later, Nagasaki is barely remembered outside of Japan as the target of the "other" bomb. Hiroshima itself exists in memory, if at all, as little more than a towering, symmetrical, even aesthetically pleasing, mushroom cloud. In the United States there has emerged an almost pathological aversion to confronting what actually took place beneath the mushroom clouds. In the phrasing of a Senate resolution of September 1994, condemning the attempt of the Smithsonian Institution to present an exhibition emphasizing the human toll in Hiroshima and Nagasaki, the bombs are said to have helped "bring World War II to a merciful end." They were the last act in a terrible conflagration, and the enormity of Japan's aggression and atrocities, the fanaticism of its resistance, made such a denouement inevitable and appropriate.

In the pages that follow here we encounter a patriotic veteran's very different view of the war and its legacy. The indiscriminate use of lethal weapons against entire populations that World War II unleashed is appalling. Mercy is nowhere to be found when listening to the story of a bereaved mother from Hiroshima or Nagasaki, or encountering a microcephalic child, stunted and malformed in the womb.

For many survivors of the bomb, the curtain never has closed on the so-called last act of the war, and never will. Dr. Yamazaki notes and calls attention to nine different forms of cancer caused by radiation exposure. Also, while there is at present no statistically significant evidence of long-term genetic effects from the bomb, the psychological trauma of fearing that this may in time emerge has been, for some victims, overwhelming. In Japanese parlance, such invisible legacies of the bomb sometimes are referred to as "keloids of the heart," "leukemia of the soul."

In Japan, the horror of Hiroshima and Nagasaki sometimes is evoked in a manner that portrays the Japanese in World War II as mere victims. The bomb, in such usage, becomes a kind of nationalism—a way of forgetting or canceling out the great suffering the Japanese caused others. To most Japanese, however, the bomb clearly transcends nationalistic history. It is only natural that they focus not on the mushroom cloud but on the human agony beneath it, and feel compelled to offer cries for sanity and peace.

That is what Dr. Yamazaki also has done, not as someone who experienced the bomb but as a physician and medical researcher who would see the world whole again. The title of his incisive memoir is both literal and figurative. He tells us what the new radioactive weapon did to its most vulnerable victims, children and even the unborn. And he reminds us that we remain, all of us, children of the atomic bomb.

ACKNOWLEDGMENTS

In a period of over five decades many individuals and organizations have made important contributions to this story. The survivors of Hiroshima and Nagasaki gave us insights into an atomic battlefield that only they can tell. We have also learned about the hazards of nuclear weapons to man and his environment from the Marshallese in the equatorial South Pacific, who were accidentally exposed to radioactive fallout.

During our tenure in Nagasaki the cordial working relationship that developed with the Nagasaki medical community was due in large measure to Dr. Raisuke Shirabe, Professor of Surgery at the Medical School. Governor Sugiyama lent his support by introducing us to his public health officials and the citizenry. Aijiro Yamaguchi, S.J., the Bishop of Nagasaki, acquainted us with the customs of Nagasaki. Some of the young physicians on the medical staff who were indispensable at ABCC and now hold prominent positions in the medical community are: Masahito Setoguchi, Atsuyoshi Takao, Shiro Tsuiki, and Sadahisa Kawamoto. Genji Matsuda later became Dean of the Nagasaki University Medical School; Michinori Hamada, an internist, took leave from his practice in Kagoshima to join the ABCC. Stanley Wright, Phyllis Wright, and Masao Kodani were our clinical and administrative associates. The pediatric staff at Hiroshima, where I was first assigned, especially Wataru Sutow and Jayne and Wayne Borges, supported our research proposals from the outset. William J. Schull was our colleague from Hiroshima who consistently made trips to Nagasaki.

Stafford L. Warren, Dean of the Medical School at the University of California at Los Angeles, allowed me to link our observation of radiation effects in Nagasaki with faculty investigations of radiation effects in early life, in particular the investigations at the Laboratory of Nuclear Medicine and Radiation Biology and the UCLA Brain Research Institute. The Stafford L. Warren Papers at the UCLA Special Collections Library provided much information about the role of medicine in the Manhattan Project (where Dr. Warren was medical director), and, most important, furnished data from investigations in Hiroshima and Nagasaki during the first months of the Allied occupation of Japan in 1945. The assistance of the Special Collections Library staff has been very helpful.

The American Academy of Pediatrics, which has a vested interest in the health and welfare of children, has played a significant role by informing its membership about the beneficent effects of radiation as well as its hazards. Drs. Robert Aldrich, Lee Farr, Paul Wehrle, Fred Silverman, and Robert W. Miller, who have been involved in this effort, have also encouraged the communication of this factual information to the general public considered in *Children of the Atomic Bomb*. Dr. John E. Mack brought to the membership his thoughts and study of the behavioral consequences of the threat of nuclear war to children.

At Marquette University considerable interest and support have been given to our project, especially by John P. Raynor, S.J., and Albert P. DiUlio, S.J., respectively past president and president of Marquette, as well as Professor Raju Thomas and Donald Kynaston.

On my return trip to Nagasaki and Hiroshima in 1989, the survivors, physicians, and the media told us of their concerns and studies of the aftermath four and a half decades later. They encouraged my proposal to write a book about their children. In Nagasaki: the Nagasaki Appeals Committee, and Drs. Tatsuichiro Akizuki, Hiroko Takahara, and Tayori Sakaguchi, former ABCC physicians;

at the Nagasaki University Medical School, Drs. Michito Ichimaru, Issei Nishimori, and Masao Kishikawa; NHK's Nagasaki broadcaster, Mr. Tatsuo Sekiguchi; Mayor Hitoshi Motoshima; at RERF Dr. J. W. Thiessen, the director, and his staff, Yoshio Okamoto, Hitoshi Tokai, and Atsuko Nakagawa. In Hiroshima: Drs. Teruaki Fukuhara and Chikako Ito of the Hiroshima Atomic Bomb Casualty Council; Katsumi Hirata of the Hiroshima Perfectural Medical Association; Mr. M. Omuta, the chief editor, and Kazuo Yabui of the *Chugoku Shinbun;* at the Radiation Effects Research Foundation, the chairman Itsuzo Shigematsu, and Drs. Seymour Abrahamson, Hiroshi Maki, and their staff; and at the Hiroshima Medical School, Dr. Kazuhiro Ueda, Professor of Pediatrics; in Tokyo: Dr. Eisei Ishikawa, who translated the medical section of *Hiroshima and Nagasaki.**

It was Cola Franzen, a poet, and Wolfgang Franzen, a professor of physics at Boston University, who not only suggested that this story be told but also patiently guided the development of the text. Dr. Elizabeth Knoll at the University of California Press, and Bill Krause, David Sischo, and Mary Sutow reviewed early drafts of the manuscript and offered invaluable suggestions for shaping the text. Hank Pizer assisted us with the presentation of the initial proposal and Beverly Liebov Sloane served as a diligent sounding board. Drs. William J. Schull and James V. Neel, the author Karen Yamashita, and the playwright Wakako Yamauchi all contributed their valuable comments. This book was written in collaboration with Louis B. Fleming, a correspondent in Italy and at the U.N. for the *Los Angeles Times.* A welcome visit from Lou in the midst of my internship at St. Louis City Hospital, soon after his enlistment in the navy and only a few months before I was called to active duty, is testimony to our long friendship and his familiarity with my life. A tour of duty at the end of World War II enabled him to see Japan at the beginning of the Allied occupation.

Discussions with John Dower, who provided many insights on the Pacific War, gave us a valuable outlook to consider. He and Professor Rinjiro Sodei introduced us to the artistry of Irie and Toshi Muraki—their depictions of the human encounter with the atomic bomb and other tragedies of World War II help fill the void where words fail. We thank John and Yasuko Dower for obtaining the drawings by the survivors that accompany this story.

We wish to thank Masao Miyoshi, Professor of Comparative Literature at the University of California at San Diego, for reviewing the manuscript and introducing us to Duke University Press. We express our gratitude to the editor, Reynolds Smith, for his backing in the publication of the book, and his associates, Pam Morrison, Sharon Parks, Mindy Conner, copy editor, Valerie Millholland, and Mark Brodsky, for their many suggestions and assistance.

At last, months late, the clinic was complete and we could begin a new examination of the children of the Nagasaki bomb, checking for the first time for effects of radiation exposure during pregnancy.

We had identified seventeen survivors for the critical study, children whose mothers had been pregnant with them when the bomb detonated at 11:02 A.M. on August 9, 1945. And their mothers had been close to the hypocenter, so close that they had developed the triad of unmistakable signs of radiation sickness: loss of hair from the scalp, painful lesions in the mouth and throat, and reddish-purple skin lesions.

I was in the small examining room. It was early May 1951. A nurse escorted in a young mother and her five-year-old son. With one glance, I knew I was seeing for the first time the terrible effect that an atomic bomb can have on the unborn. I concealed my feelings and proceeded with a routine pediatric examination. Finally, tape measure in hand, I confirmed the reduced head size. His erratic and uncontrolled behavior was evidence that mental retardation was also present.

These were the very symptoms we had expected on the basis of what was known about incidental radiation exposure to the fetuses of mothers being treated for cancer. But that did not lessen the impact of seeing this first case among the survivors of the Nagasaki bomb.

Four other pediatricians were working with me on the clinical examinations. We conferred repeatedly, trying to be sure that we had

as complete a diagnosis as possible. We also knew the importance of
caution. We did not want to create panic or unjustified fears in the
already traumatized populations of Nagasaki and Hiroshima. Much
more work would be required to determine the precise role of the
bomb in these abnormalities.

I recall adopting an objective, cautious posture a few weeks later
when I met with a visiting medical team from the Atomic Energy
Commission. "We need a careful review of the records and assessment of the findings of such grave consequences to the unborn prior
to the publication of the data," I said. They agreed.

That appraisal and that assessment were to be my challenge as I
prepared to leave Nagasaki after completing my work as physician
in charge for the Atomic Bomb Casualty Commission.

I had come to Nagasaki just over four years after the bomb. With
me were my wife, Aki, and our young son, Paul. And a million perplexing questions. The biggest question, of course, was what on earth
a pediatrician, trained to make children whole, could do in the aftermath of this terrible, terrible devastation of a generation of children.
How could I deal with the anomaly of being a Japanese American
who had served in the U.S. Army in the war just finished, had been
a prisoner of war in Germany, had never before set foot on the
land of his ancestors, and came now during the massive American
occupation?

I did not know, as I prepared to leave, that my twenty-month
sojourn in Nagasaki was just the beginning of an involvement with
the children of the atomic bomb that would extend through the rest
of my life. I would have been troubled indeed had I known then that
some of the answers would remain elusive fifty years after the bombs
were detonated.

1 NAGASAKI

We were not prepared for the contrasts of Nagasaki.

An enormous military-industrial complex had been developed there before the outbreak of World War II, with factories stretching for miles in a valley that opens to the south where the rest of the city spreads around the head of a spacious protected harbor. Mountains rise sharply, some more than two thousand feet above the valley floor, dividing the city—separating, as the local inhabitants would discover in August 1945, the living from the dead. Some of Japan's largest battleships, including the dreadnought *Musashi*, were built here. Other makers of the tools of war lined the banks of the Urakami River as it flows to the beautiful harbor.

A second valley lies east of the main mountain spur, shielded by the mountains of Nishiyama and Nakagawa so that even this bomb, the most powerful ever unleashed on a living target, had only limited impact. The tranquil beauty of this valley and the graceful bridges that span the Nakashima River have long been celebrated by the artists of Japan.

And just to the southeast lies the place where we lived on the side of Atagoyama mountain. It was a world almost untouched by the bomb, a world still tied closely to its past, with roadside views of Mogi Bay below, where traditional fishermen worked as they had for centuries and seaside restaurants served the more affluent residents of Nagasaki.

There is a history of ties to the Western world unique to Nagasaki. This was the first port of entry for the Portuguese when Japan was opened to them in 1571. The Dutch maintained a foothold on Deshima in the bay when the rest of Japan was sealed off from the outside world by the Foreign Exclusion Act in 1636. The Dutch brought modern medicine to Japan through Nagasaki. Roman Catholic priests, despite persecution, maintained a Christian hold within the city, and their followers were among those who suffered the most in the bombing.

But this mixture of contrasts and historical contradictions only served to bewilder me when we arrived that January day in 1950. There had been no briefings. I was the only American doctor. My assignment as chief physician of the Atomic Bomb Casualty Commission (ABCC) in Nagasaki had been thrust on me after my arrival in Japan. I had accepted reluctantly, always suspecting that it was a form of exile because I had protested the racial discrimination my family and I had suffered from the British occupation officers in Hiroshima.

I did not have time to reflect on my anxieties, however. From the moment of my arrival, I sensed the need to get busy. The first thing to do was to deal with the inevitable hostility of people still overwhelmed with anger after the bombing. Many survivors thought we had come to use them simply as guinea pigs,[1] and that our sole interest was to gain information to protect Americans in the United States in the event of an atomic attack. They were skeptical about our real concern for their well-being. They doubted that there would be any treatment for those suffering the long-term effects of radiation.

Somehow, urgently, I had to gain their confidence, assure them that we were genuinely concerned about their well-being and were not there to treat them as experimental laboratory animals.

But how to proceed?

Although I had never been in Japan before, I knew from my mother and father and grandmother of the respect for tradition and authority that is part of Japanese culture. I have a feeling that the

assertiveness training I received as a youthful encyclopedia sales-
man in Los Angeles also facilitated my work, balancing my respect
for the Japanese culture as I struggled to initiate our work.

Japan was then administered through forty-six regions, called
prefectures, in addition to the three municipal administrations in
Tokyo, Osaka, and Kyoto. General Douglas MacArthur, supreme
commander of the Allied powers (SCAP), who was overseeing the
occupation, worked through the prefectural governors. If he did, I
realized, then so should I.

Governor Sugiyama headed the Nagasaki prefectural government.
I can only imagine the stresses he must have suffered, governing that
ravaged people, rebuilding the shattered economy. But none of this
showed in his friendly, charismatic personality, in the warmth with
which he greeted me. He assured me of his support and assistance
with one proviso: We would get along well only if we recognized
that Americans and Japanese approached situations differently and
expressed themselves in different ways. As soon as he said this, he
broke out in hearty, disarming laughter. But he was certainly correct.

And he was true to his word. He was accessible when problems
arose. He introduced me to his staff. It was particularly reassuring to
have this good relationship, for he was also our landlord. The ABCC
had taken over the lease on the Kaikan Building, owned by the pre-
fecture, and it was there that we would establish the first clinics to
examine children for the effects of bomb radiation.

The governor reached out in unofficial ways as well. He had been
introducing me to his staff with stag parties in restaurants and geisha
houses. The only women present on these occasions were the geishas, who helped serve and entertained with their traditional dances.
I felt too insecure to suggest an alternative. Nor did I have the nerve
to tell him of the understandable annoyance of my wife, Aki, with
this men-only entertaining. But somehow he heard of Aki's displea-
sure. Thereupon Mrs. Sugiyama arrived at our home to visit Aki, and

she and Aki were both included at the governor's next dinner party, to the evident astonishment of the ever-present geishas.

Who should I see next? I decided it should be the chief of police. What a fortuitous decision that proved to be, more useful than I could have imagined. For it was he who first taught me about the human impact of the bomb.

It is hard for me to believe today how little I knew then about the bomb and its devastation. There had already been a thorough and authoritative survey of the short-term medical impact of the two bombs on the people of Hiroshima and Nagasaki. But the reports were all classified, and none of their contents had been made available to me.

Even though I had served as a combat officer in the U.S. Army in the European Theater, was on special assignment for the ABCC, and had security clearance from the Atomic Energy Commission, I was told nothing. I did not even know of the existence of these reports until shortly before I left Japan. Certainly no reference was made to them in the interviews I had with the principal scientists in the investigation before I came to Japan. It would have been immensely helpful to have had access to these findings as we groped our way toward establishing our research on the effects of the radiation.

There has never been an official explanation of the secrecy. I think it may have stemmed from a desire to avoid greater backlash from the Japanese themselves if the full story of the bombs' effects on people, especially children, had been told at that time. There certainly was a determination among the American authorities then to suppress most of the relevant information. Even the press coverage was severely censored under rules of the occupation.

So I first learned the human dimensions of the Nagasaki bomb from Chief of Police Deguchi. He had been an assistant chief of air raid defense for the prefectural police department when the bomb exploded.

"Tell me about it," I said, trying to conceal my vast ignorance of the bomb's impact on the population.

He was alive and able to tell the story only because the building where he was working at the time, Katsuyama Primary School, was protected by the mountain ridge that separates the Urakami and Nishiyama Valleys.

There had been an air raid alarm earlier that morning, but no bombs fell. Some people had come out of shelters as eleven o'clock approached, only to hear the distant throb of bomber engines. Before many could take cover again, there was a flash of extremely bright light, blinding even on the far side of the mountain ridge, then a thunderous blast that shook the school building for a full minute, followed by terrifying darkness as the atomic cloud eclipsed the sun.

Deguchi ordered a police patrol to find out what had happened on the other side of the ridge. The policemen were back in minutes. The industrial area was engulfed in flames, they said, thousands appeared dead, and the survivors were running in panic, many of them left with only burning shreds of their clothing. The railroad station, a quarter of a mile away, was destroyed. Health services were paralyzed with the destruction of the University Medical Center. The new prefectural offices had burned to the ground. The fires were spreading.

Three hours later, the first refugees from the Urakami Valley struggled around and over the ridge to reach the Katsuyama School where Deguchi was working. They collapsed in utter shock. No organized rescue effort had been possible in the first hours. Rescue teams from the navy hospitals that tried to enter the Urakami Valley on the first day were driven back by a wall of flame. Trucks and trains were able to transport those escaping to the north, but many died in the crowded vehicles before they ever reached neighboring towns.

On the second day, rescue workers were able to enter the city even

On August 9, 1945, at 11:02 A.M., there was a blinding, searing light, and then the sky over Nagasaki became blacker than night. The dust and debris from the atomic bomb explosion blanketed Urakami Valley, completely blocking out the sun. U.S. Army-Air Force photo HQ AAF/AS-2. From Stafford L. Warren Papers, 987, Box 62, Folder 7, UCLA Special Collections Library.

The map of Nagasaki (right) shows the location of the hypocenter, equidistant from the two principal military-industrial complexes and disastrously close to the medical center.

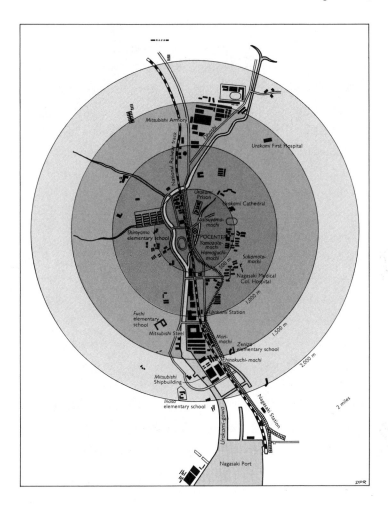

though huge fires continued to burn. They found some survivors in the smoldering ruins and brought them to emergency centers.

Dealing with families proved the hardest task, Chief Deguchi told me. Parents and children, separated at the time of the bomb, struggled to find survivors in their families. They had no way to know who had survived. Days would pass before they could find out.

Over the next three days, the police began to gather the dead. The bodies of those who could be identified were turned over to relatives, who had joined the search. Those who could not be identified were cremated, the ashes buried in common graves. Two weeks were required to remove all of the dead from the Urakami Valley.

"The first reports to Tokyo were that there had been no serious damage," Chief Deguchi told me. In fact, every part of the city had suffered some damage, ranging from broken windows in outlying areas to incineration at the hypocenter. From the minute the bomb detonated, there was general despair, he said. As the hours passed and the extent of the damage of that single bomb became clearer, there was a growing realization that resistance to the Western Allies by Japan was no longer possible.

As I heard this report I began to question whether we would ever find survivors who could help us discover the medical lessons of this incredible exposure to radiation. The trauma, both physical and psychological, obviously had been universal.

The experience of the chief of police filled enormous gaps in my knowledge and showed me how much more I had to learn. The time obviously had come to make contact with the medical community. But before that, I knew I must see what the bomb had done. I asked our staff driver to take me in the commission's Jeep to the places most affected by the bomb — places that would enable me to match the stories of the survivors with the remains of their city.

We started at the northern extremity of the industrial complex, where torpedoes were manufactured, and then worked our way south to visit the shattered Roman Catholic church, the University Medical School, and the University Hospital.

Nothing had been done to restore the industrial plants. At the Mitsubishi torpedo works, on the west bank of the Urakami River, I left the Jeep and walked alone on the vast concrete slab floors. There were no walls, no roofs. But rows of machine tools remained bolted to the flooring, and skeletal structures twisted almost beyond recognition above, where once workers had thronged.

Casting shop at the Mitsubishi steel and arms works, three quarters of a mile from the hypocenter. Photo by Shigeo Hayashi.

We crossed the river to get a closer look at the Catholic church, which overlooked the valley from the foothills just east of the factory belt. And we drove past the University Medical Center, now etched on the hillside like a fortress ravaged in an unimaginable battle.

There was, of course, a missing dimension. The dead, the dying, the blistered survivors, and the victims in frantic flight were long since gone. There remained only the backdrop of a macabre stage set. Yet I could almost see the desperate people so vividly described by the police chief as I looked over the scene that afternoon, knowing how much clearer it would become as I continued to hear the stories of those who had been here.

Finally, with a deep sense of anxiety, I asked the driver to take me to the hypocenter. We descended from the higher land, where the university and hospital stand, to the flat area immediately east of the river. A small tributary joins the Urakami River just beyond that point. There we came to a small garden with a bench for visitors, a small berm at the center. Shrubs had been neatly planted on the periphery, but it was a cold winter day and no flowers bloomed.

On the small rise was a wooden column, simply marked "Hypocenter." Five hundred and fifty yards overhead, the bomb had exploded. The toll was tallied on a placard at the side: 76,796 killed.

No one was there when I made my visit. There was silence, the distant throb of city life somehow erased. I felt as if I were attending a gigantic wake, alone. It was not easy to pull myself away. But I knew it was time to go home, to the other world to which I returned each evening.

So we turned our backs on the gutted industrial area and left behind the shattered hillside buildings, retreating to the solace of the house where Aki and I lived, screened by a mountain from this horror.

At the end of that short drive there was no sign of the war. Our house had been requisitioned from a wealthy businessman for our use. It was a gem of a house sitting within a pristine, carefully manicured garden that screened out any signs of the atomic destruction. We did not look out on desolation or war damage. On the contrary, our view was of the verdant garden, rich in color even in its winter foliage, with a delicate bridge arching over a quiet pond, neatly trimmed grass, and beds where azaleas, lilies, irises, and camellias soon would bloom.

We lived, in effect, on an island that had escaped the ferocity of the explosion because it was hidden behind the ridge of the mountains that border the valley—mountains that arbitrated who would survive in the milliseconds after the detonation. I returned there each evening, grateful for the seclusion. But Aki and I never overcame the unease of occupying someone else's dwelling, of seeing the owner come, from time to time, to look at his garden. We knew in very personal ways the pain a family feels when it is displaced.

That evening, after seeing for the first time the physical damage caused by the bomb, I felt a new urgency to establish ties with the doctors of Nagasaki, and through them, with the children of Nagasaki.

My anxiety at the time would have been eased had I known of the total cooperation I would receive in the months ahead from physicians, from parents, from the children themselves. And I would learn that being a Japanese American would make no difference.

2 BORN IN AMERICA

My father and mother were born in Japan, but I was a native Californian with a total sense of belonging to America. My brothers and sister and I always thought of ourselves as Americans. I recited the Pledge of Allegiance with commitment and fervor as I worked my way up to Eagle Scout. I sang "My country 'tis of thee, sweet land of liberty." Our family celebrated Thanksgiving with turkey and all the fixings, even if we felt a little distant from the culture of the Pilgrims and Plymouth Rock.

Yet, through all those years of growing up, when I had no doubt that I was indeed an American, I was inevitably called a Japanese by the population at large. Ironically, when I came to Japan for the first time at the age of thirty-three, the Japanese had no doubt about who I was. I was not one of them. I was an American.

That paradox touched the lives of everyone in my family. My father had been denied citizenship under the racist American immigration laws, but his love and support for the United States did not flag, even when he was forced into a relocation camp during World War II. Such was his patriotic fervor that he was beaten in the relocation camp by frustrated parents because he urged their Japanese-American sons to enlist in the U.S. Army.

My military service would have been in jeopardy had not my army commission arrived a week before the Japanese attacked Pearl Harbor. My application for military service had been filed shortly after beginning my medical studies, but there was a long delay while the War Department sought to verify my citizenship.

As a child, because of my father's citizenship, I had been given dual Japanese and American citizenship. But my father had clarified my status as an American citizen by renouncing the Japanese citizenship of his children in 1932. He never explained his decision. I am sure that, essentially, he wanted to demonstrate his commitment to raise his children as American citizens; it may also have reflected his misgivings about the growing militarism in Japan.

The army conducted a lengthy investigation before confirming my claim of American citizenship.[2] Had the result been delayed another week, I would have found myself, like so many other Japanese Americans, a person without a country. In the reaction to the Japanese attack on the United States, rules were adopted in Washington to deny the rights of citizenship to those of Japanese ancestry, although similar rules were rarely enacted against Americans tracing their ancestry to the other two enemy nations, Germany and Italy.

One of my brothers and I were both in the armed forces of the United States when the rest of our family was taken away to concentration camps during the massive relocation of Japanese and Japanese Americans from the West Coast in April 1942.[3] They were allowed to take along only what they could carry: eating utensils, bedding, and personal effects.

We have never forgotten that our friends in the Japanese-American community of Hawaii were largely exempt from that outrageous action. Of the 185,000 people of Japanese ancestry in Hawaii at the time, fewer than 2,000 were taken into custody. But all of them were placed under martial law and denied their basic constitutional rights, an action struck down in 1946 by the Supreme Court.[4] The loyal cooperation of the Hawaiians of Japanese ancestry with military and defense authorities more than justified the decision to permit most of them to stay. And it underscored the injustice of the treatment of the West Coast population.

I must be careful not to give the impression that my family engaged in angry protest or was embittered by the discriminatory ex-

periences that touched Asians in the United States before and during
World War II. The reparations enacted by Congress, the token pay-
ment long after the war to the families affected by the relocation,
have helped heal those wounds. Even on that issue, however, I was
not actively engaged. My father, John Yamazaki, would have been
the last to lead a protest march. He deeply regretted the relocation,
but he was also worried about the likelihood of violence against
Japanese Americans had they remained on the West Coast.

He was a schoolteacher in the foothills of the Japanese alps in
Nagano Province when he set out to learn to be a doctor in San
Francisco in 1904 at the age of twenty. He survived the earthquake
of 1906.

My father's interest in medicine was diverted to a growing concern
for the immigrant population, and he began working at an Episcopal mission on Pine Street. He converted to Christianity, something
he felt compelled to keep secret from his Buddhist family in Japan
at the time. Ultimately he was sponsored for training at a seminary
in New Haven, Connecticut. He became a priest and the vicar of
St. Mary's Episcopal Church in Los Angeles, where he continued to
serve until his death at the age of 101.

Before he left Japan he met my mother, Mary Tsune Tanaka, a
student in a Christian high school in Matsumoto. By the time of his
departure they had agreed that one day they would be married. I
do not know how much of the traditional family participation was
involved in that matchmaking.

My mother must have been perplexed when ten years went by
without any action by my father, in distant America, to claim her. At
that point, Mary Louise Patterson, who had been head of the high
school in Matsumoto, took matters into her own hands. From her
home in Los Angeles she sent Mary the passage money to America.
Then she escorted my father to meet his betrothed in San Francisco. He had to borrow money from a friend for his rail ticket.

The Yamazaki family, ca. 1918, in front of the rectory next door to St. Mary's Church. Left to right: James Nobuo; father, John Misao; John Henry Michio; mother, Mary Tsune; and Peter Tamio.

They proceeded directly from the pier to Grace Cathedral for their wedding.

The bride and groom went immediately to Los Angeles, where my father already had taken up his ministry at St. Mary's. They were to live out their lives in the rectory at 960 South Normandie Avenue, next door to St. Mary's Church at 961 South Mariposa Avenue.

My closest link to Japan during my school years was my grandmother, who came from Japan to live with us when I was five and remained for the last ten years of her life. She spoke no English, creating a challenge to us to preserve some knowledge of the Japanese language. I at least had that resource when I reached Japan.

She was rich in the traditions, the charming folk tales of old Japan, stories that came back to me later in Nagasaki. And she always found solace in her pipe, with its long bamboo stem and its thimble-size bronzed tip, which she filled with finely shredded tobacco.

A clergyman father can be quite demanding. He insisted that each of us help care for the parish, with responsibilities ranging from janitorial duties to escorting young people to summer camp. Both he and Mother believed that their example, rather than their preaching, was the best way to teach us. But if we were overcome by the injustice of having to work so hard, my father would take us to an orphanage he had helped establish in the Silver Lake district of Los Angeles and let us simply observe children who would have given anything to change places with us.

The most severe scoldings we received from my father came when we returned home later than expected from a date. It was not that he was worried about what we might have been doing; he just hated to be delayed in his departure, in our one family automobile, for the deep-sea fishing he cherished. He would drive to the beach shortly after midnight and board a commercial fishing boat with dozens of other enthusiasts for a dawn fishing expedition.

St. Mary's was in what was called Uptown in Los Angeles, a neighborhood bounded by Vermont and Western, and by Pico and San Marino Streets, including a section of Tenth Street, now Olympic Boulevard, lined with a concentration of Japanese stores. The population of Uptown was predominantly of Japanese ancestry. Most of us went to the neighborhood public schools and Los Angeles High School.

What a comfortable place it was to grow up in, knowing almost everybody in the neighborhood, welcome in shops and homes alike. My mother loved people, and she visited around the neighborhood with great energy. She always made a particular point of taking tea with any family that might be the object of criticism or unpopularity. And her teapot at home was always ready for anyone who came by, from parishioners to the grocery delivery man.

Uptown was, in a sense, a ghetto, and it was the target from time to time of bigotry. But we were largely oblivious to those prejudices and our isolation until we started looking for jobs. The employment office at the Ambassador Hotel, three blocks from my home, ordered me to leave by the back service door when I had the temerity to apply for a job. About the only jobs we could get were as assistants to the Japanese-American gardeners who made up a large part of the local population. My brother Peter and I worked three summers on farms in the Imperial Valley and at Watsonville, starkly aware of how much worse off were most of those laboring with us.

We were not allowed to swim at a commercial pool a bike ride away. The principal at Los Angeles High excluded us from the senior prom, so we arranged a substitute event in the parish hall at St. Mary's.

The hostility many felt toward the Japanese and Japanese Americans came sharply home to us when some community groups organized to try, unsuccessfully, to block the expansion of St. Mary's. Only through a court order was my father able to go ahead with the project. John and I made dawn patrols to remove inflammatory posters that were regularly mounted in the neighborhood, warning that property values would fall if the church expansion proceeded. A member of the state legislature was a prime opponent, exploiting racist feelings to increase his own popularity.

I recall no bitterness on my father's part in the face of the discrimination and racism. He never seemed daunted by the number of opponents or critics. He would urge us, over and over, to count the number of our supporters, not our enemies. "Remember how many friends you have," he would say.

During my high school years I became increasingly aware of Japan's military expansionism on the Asian mainland. I spent time at the Los Angeles Public Library reading about the aggression in Manchuria, which was denounced by the League of Nations. I can still see the newsreel and newspaper photographs of the Japanese ambassador, Yosuke Matsuoka, stalking out of the League of Nations in 1933. Increasing numbers of Japanese were emigrating to Manchuria at that time of deep world economic depression. Their favorite destinations, the United States and Australia, had closed their doors. Newspaper cartoons at the time had hideous caricatures of Japanese military leaders. More and more, there was talk of the "yellow peril" as Japan expanded into Shanghai.

As a high school student my goal was to go on to the University of California at Los Angeles — UCLA. I succeeded, and it could not have been a better experience. It was there that I was guided to premed courses. I would, years later, come back to UCLA to teach and to continue my research on the impact of the atomic bomb on the children of Nagasaki. To this day I remain deeply impressed with the quality of education offered at this great state-funded institution.

I was toying with two careers: medicine and oceanography. My decision was narrowed after a day spent floating offshore of the Scripps Institute of Oceanography at La Jolla. As the vessel lurched, rolled, and pitched, I was overtaken by seasickness, ready to swim ashore rather than suffer another minute afloat. Little did I know that I would be seaborne again in just a few years, first bound for the European theater, and then for my medical assignment in Japan.

As my interest in medicine increased, so did my realization of the difficulty of gaining admission to a medical school. It was difficult for everyone, of course, but there was a particular problem for me: I was of Oriental extraction.

We premeds struggled to keep our grade point averages high. And those of us of Asian ancestry maintained a private research program, examining the lists of students accepted at each medical school, counting the Asian names to get a hint of where we were most likely to be accepted.

Ivan Baronofsky, with whom I had studied in an experimental embryology laboratory at UCLA, had become a teaching assistant at Marquette University, a Jesuit institution in Milwaukee. He urged me to apply there. I was encouraged by his own victory over discrimination, for he had won his appointment despite the quotas many universities applied to the admission of Jews.

His was good advice. I was accepted, and I relished the training. And my father at least had the satisfaction of having a son graduate as a medical doctor even though his own dreams of a career in medicine were not realized.

My family faced hard sacrifices to make my medical training possible. My older brother, John, was already enrolled in the Divinity School of the Pacific in Berkeley, preparing to become, like my father, a priest in the Episcopal church. My younger brother, Peter, agreed to postpone law school. And my sister, Louise, still in high school, faced a greater burden of helping at home.

Financial matters became even worse when my parents and sister were forced to relocate to a concentration camp. They had no income. And Peter, who had enlisted in the army when the attack on Pearl Harbor occurred, had only a private's pay.

History, at least, has set the record straight about the loyalty of the Japanese-American population during World War II. More than thirty thousand Nisei served in the U.S. Armed Forces. The exploits of the Nisei in the 100th/442d Regimental Combat Team set an unequaled standard for heroism. More than six thousand Nisei graduated from the intelligence school at Camp Savage and Fort Snelling in Minnesota and played an immensely important role, particularly in the Pacific war that ultimately defeated Japan. "They are our human secret weapons," President Harry S Truman had said, adding, "The role that 6,000 Japanese-American soldiers played in the Pacific Battlefields has been a well kept secret until now."

Our loyalty was never in doubt. The woman who later would become my wife, Aki Hirasahiki, had been among the UCLA students who declared, three days after Pearl Harbor, "None of us have known loyalty to any country other than America, and in the face of our ancestral country's unwarranted attack upon the country of our birth, we wholeheartedly desire to renew our pledge of faith in the United States."

Her father, who ran a wholesale produce business in Los Angeles, had been taken from his home on Pearl Harbor night by FBI agents and was held for months in federal detention centers at Terminal Island and in Montana. The reason? He was suspected of disloyalty because he had donated $25 to an entertainment fund for visiting Japanese midshipmen at Los Angeles. When the charges were finally dropped, he was allowed to join his family in one of the relocation camps. A simple act of hospitality had been interpreted as treason. Aki's relocation terminated her studies at UCLA. Fifty years later, university officials at last made amends when they awarded her the degree she had lost in the hysteria after Pearl Harbor was attacked.

My parents took great pride in what their children accomplished. John was honored as a canon in the Episcopal Diocese of Los Angeles. Peter's long service in the army in the occupation of Japan led to a career in business rather than the law. Louise had a distinguished career as a social worker. She had earned her bachelor's degree at Carleton College once she was released from the relocation camp and before she was allowed to return to California. Later she earned a master's degree in social work at the University of Southern California.

I have great respect for the work my father did, and for the work my brother John did as his successor at St. Mary's. Religion never became a part of my life as I matured. But my father was sure I would "see the light" one day.

In many ways, our family was the immigrant dream come true. But it was a dream with its nightmare dimension as the family was caught up in the confusion and abuse that followed Pearl Harbor.

On that Sunday morning, December 7, 1941, I was seated at my desk in Ma Brown's boardinghouse on 16th Street, just around the corner from Wisconsin Avenue, in Milwaukee. My old Philco, with its low-fidelity four-inch speaker, was tuned down to filter in soft background music as I reviewed class notes.

Two years earlier, my former UCLA colleague, Ivan Baronofsky, had met me at the train and escorted me to Ma Brown's. I could still remember my arrival — climbing the stairs, hearing the landlady's hearty laughter and the loud jokes of some of her boarders, and wondering how I could study amid such noise and confusion. But the price was right: $50 a month, meals included. And Ma Brown's Irish warmth and mirth, her generous servings of meat and potatoes, created a home away from home that could not be matched anywhere else in Milwaukee. I was enjoying the comfort of my room that lazy Sunday morning, lulled by the quiet music on the radio. It must have been about noon.

Suddenly, the music was interrupted. An excited voice was reading an urgent news bulletin. Pearl Harbor, bastion of the United States Navy in the Pacific, was under attack. Japanese planes were bombing the vast complex, the harbor, the adjacent airfields.

I sat frozen at my desk. And as the meaning of the news became clearer, as its implications gained hold in my mind, I thought the future dark indeed.

Half of my medical training had been completed. I had received my army commission just a week before. Now, the war I thought we would fight only in Europe had spread to the Pacific.

For Americans of Japanese ancestry it was a time of particular shock. I do not know if German Americans and Italian Americans felt the same horror as the nations of their parents were taken over by expansionist military regimes.

My brother John, just ordained, was celebrating Holy Communion at St. Mary's for a congregation made up almost entirely of Japanese immigrants and their children. A friend who heard the report on his radio rushed to the church with the news.

My father, as president of the Southern California Japanese Church Federation, convened the Christian ministers of the area within hours. They designed an elaborate support plan for their parishioners, support that would extend until the people were taken away to the relocation centers and camps. In many cases, the ministers accompanied their flocks into the camps.

But I could not imagine, that first day, the dire consequences that awaited my own family as the hysteria inspired by Pearl Harbor spread. I am sure I was thinking more of the short-term impact. How would my country recover from and respond to this devastating treachery? And, in a very personal sense, how would this affect the completion of my training as a physician?

It was that very night that the FBI swept through Uptown, Los Angeles, arresting, among others, Aki's father. And it was then that the FBI began careful surveillance of the rectory at St. Mary's. Louise reported that my mother became expert at identifying the agents among the callers at the church and would quietly say to other family members: "F-san at the door."

An FBI agent called on me at Ma Brown's as well. He had come to confirm my father's statement about my army commission.

I have said that I was not religious, despite the internal strength I gained growing up in a church family. But in those days, I would walk down Wisconsin Avenue, the principal thoroughfare of Mil-

waukee, to kneel in the Gesu Church, which was the chapel for
Marquette University as well as a parish church. Perhaps it helped.
I was not, however, able to overcome my doubts about the power of
divine guidance, nor could I find the abiding faith that sustained my
parents and my brother John.

Reassuring word soon reached me from the army. I would be permitted to continue my studies; my commission would not be with-
drawn. And my coursework would be accelerated so that I would
receive my medical degree three months ahead of schedule in February 1943.

The final two years of my training opened my eyes to the challenge
of pediatrics and led me toward the specialized work I would later
undertake—work that would take me to Nagasaki and the children
of the bomb.

This early training was concentrated at the Milwaukee County
General Hospital and the Children's Hospital, just a block away from
Ma Brown's. Our dean, Dr. Eben J. Carey, was dedicated to training
general practitioners, a policy that helped me greatly in subsequent
years both as a combat physician and when I worked among the
atomic bomb survivors.

The training included a month of home-delivery obstetrics in
nearby Chicago, on the South Side, a forlorn and troubled area
served heroically by the Chicago Maternity Center. The crime and
violence in the area forced police to patrol in groups of three. Two
student doctors were dispatched on each call. The wartime shortage
of physicians and nurses made it impossible to provide further support. We had specially equipped medical bags and the encouraging
words of our mentors, nothing more.

I was relaxing after one of those deliveries, chatting with the
family of the new arrival in the living room of their modest apartment, when there was a frantic cry from a woman who had been
helping the young mother. "Doctor, Doctor," she called. I ran into
the bedroom just in time to receive a second baby. The prenatal ex-

aminations had failed to discover that she was carrying twins. I took no chances after that.

My most discouraging experience came one night in a darkened building on a narrow side street. We rang the bell, and a minute later a sliding slot opened in the door and a harsh voice called out, "What do you want?" I held up the obstetrics bag, and the door was opened. It was a brothel. On a simple metal cot in a side room, a youngster, perhaps fifteen or sixteen years old, was ready for delivery.

We delivered the baby. Then, the other student and I routinely reviewed emergency procedures for the new mother, gave telephone numbers to a woman in attendance, and promised that a nurse would be by for a checkup in a day or two. Despite the squalor, both mother and baby appeared well. But we knew the slim chances both had for a full and rewarding life.

We both felt concern for the whole child, not just its physical health, and for the whole family. It is a concern that grows with any practice of medicine, especially when the practice touches the lives of children. It was a concern that led me to specialize in pediatrics after I returned from the war in Europe. It was a concern that would accompany me to Nagasaki.

Graduation came a month after my obstetrics assignment in Chicago. It was an event toward which I had been building, training, and working for twenty years. But as matters developed, it was a lonely and isolated occasion, robbed of much of the sense of celebration, for no one in my family could be present. All of them but one brother were still incarcerated in the American concentration camps.

Peter was a buck private in the army. He had left law school immediately after Pearl Harbor to enlist. As a soldier of Japanese ancestry, he had been given the options of cleaning bedpans or washing dishes. He chose dishwashing in the officers' mess. It was not long, however, before he was commissioned. Later, when the war was won, he went to Japan as an intelligence officer.

Just before graduation I received a gift that was to change my life. It was a beautiful leather-covered clock from Abercrombie & Fitch in New York. There was no gift card, but I speculated. It must have come from Aki, who by then had been released from the relocation camp to live with her sister in New York. Who else? I was wrong, as it turned out. But the unexpected consequences of my guess were wonderful. The clock was a gift that led to my marriage with Aki. I learned many years later that it was from my brother John. He was in a relocation camp in Arizona pending a possible assignment as a military chaplain and had ordered it from a catalogue.

There were three weeks of vacation between graduation and my new assignment as an intern at City Hospital in St. Louis. First came the reluctant farewells to Ma Brown and those who had shared the warmth of her hospitality for those four years. It was then that I was able to visit my parents and Louise at Camp Jerome and see firsthand how thousands of West Coast Japanese and Japanese Americans had been treated.

The awful conditions in which my family were imprisoned seemed distant and vague before this personal visit. I took a train from Chicago to an unscheduled stop in Arkansas. It was the middle of the night. I stepped down from the train in a glare of searchlights. An officer with a detachment of armed soldiers asked for my identification, then drove me in a Jeep to nearby Camp Jerome, visible long before we arrived because of the bright lights on the guard towers. I was escorted through gates into the barbed wire enclosure.

But we did not proceed to the barracks. To my shock, we went instead to the camp hospital, where my father was recovering from a massive beating. His swollen face and bruised body bore witness to the viciousness of the attack. He was grateful only that his attackers removed his glasses before one pinned his arms behind him and the others pummeled his small and wiry frame.

"Don't worry, James," he said immediately. "I am all right." Eager

Rev. Yamazaki Was Beaten in Camp, 1943, oil on canvas by Henry Sugimoto. When Rev. Yamazaki acted as a Japanese language translator for a loyalty questionnaire administered in February 1943, he was thought to be an agent of the U.S. government and therefore responsible for the ensuing separation of "loyal" and "disloyal" inmates. The painting is unusual in its representation of the tension and divisions within the camp. Courtesy of the Japanese American National Museum, Los Angeles.

to show me that his injuries were not serious, he moved on the hospital bed and smiled weakly, but I could see the terrible pain that accompanied each movement.

I was able to reassure my mother and sister the next morning that the injuries were not life threatening and that, without major complications, Father would recover. At age sixty-one, he was a most resilient patient.

Perhaps I should not have been surprised by this brutal event. A few weeks earlier, I had received word in a letter from friends that my father was in danger. After the beating he declined to identify his assailants. He understood, I am sure, that the attack was a measure of the deep frustration felt by so many imprisoned in those relocation camps.

My father's vigorous counsel to the young men that they should enlist in the army only increased the anger of some who had seen their military draft eligibility changed from 1-A to 4-C, unfit for military service. Although American citizens, they had been dispossessed of their homes and incarcerated in what they understood to be a total deprivation of their constitutional rights.

I stayed on in Camp Jerome for more than a week, occupying my father's bed in a small tar-papered barracks room, eating with Mother and Louise in the mess hall, visiting old friends from Uptown, Los Angeles. As a visiting doctor, I was invited to give a lecture on poisonous snakes, one of the environmental hazards of the camp. It was the first time I had put my undergraduate interest in herpetology to practical use.

As soon as I arrived in St. Louis I was assigned to the Contagious Disease Hospital, which was struggling to respond to an outbreak of a virulent form of meningitis. There I learned an important lesson about the limits of what a doctor can do, a lesson that returned to me when I met the physicians who served the survivors of the Nagasaki and Hiroshima bombs: However good our training, however miraculous the drugs we have, we cannot always prevent death.

Our only effective response to the meningitis was intravenous applications of a recently introduced drug, sulfa. We medicated ourselves as well in the hope that the sulfa would also serve as a preventive. It was grim work, and exhausting, but most helpful in my education. Spinal taps became routine as we ministered to these critically ill patients. Two facts stood out at the Contagious Disease Hospital: All of the St. Louis hospitals were racially segregated except this one, and at this one, the great majority of nurses who volunteered for the tough work were African Americans.

I learned a second important lesson in St. Louis: the efficacy of another new drug, the antibiotic penicillin. It was in extremely short supply then, and cases were carefully screened before its use was approved. I presented the case of one of my patients, a man with life-threatening lung abscesses, and won approval. His response to the penicillin was dramatic. It saved his life. The case was carefully catalogued to become part of the accumulating data that would facilitate effective use of the drug. In a few months, when I found myself in combat, I would fully appreciate the importance of sulfa and penicillin.

The interns in St. Louis learned yet another lesson while I was there, but it had nothing to do with medicine. After years of hardship they had finally revolted against the parsimonious pay and endless hours. The City Council responded with a pay raise, to $50 a month, equivalent to the pay of an apprentice seaman in the navy at that time. But the hospital administrator had his own response. He quickly raised our pay to the new standard but began charging for room and board. Our take-home pay fell to below $25 a month. Only those lucky at informal gambling games found themselves with enough cash for a night on the town.

One of my last visitors before I left St. Louis was Lieutenant Kei Tanahashi, a classmate at UCLA. He had been an officer in the ROTC at UCLA and had volunteered for the service while in the relocation center at Poston, Arizona. He was off to join the 100th/442d Regimental Combat Team of Japanese Americans bound for Europe. "We'll show them," he told me as he left. They did. And he did, a member of what President Truman was to call "the most decorated unit in United States military history." But Kei was one of those who did not come home.

When my father recovered from the injuries he received in the relocation center, he and my mother were allowed to leave, but not to return to Los Angeles. They found a small apartment in Chicago. My sister was able to go to college. And I was able to visit my parents in that apartment after finishing my internship. I had my first job as a doctor during that brief time. I worked at an induction center, providing physical examinations for volunteers and draftees.

Knowing my departure was imminent, my mother had been hurriedly knitting a *hara-maki*, a waistband worn by the soldiers of Japan that symbolizes the umbilical tie of the warrior to his mother. I confess that I never felt like a warrior when I found myself in the heat of battle. But I cherished the symbol.

I was with my parents in that Chicago apartment, far from their home in Los Angeles, when my active duty orders arrived. I was to proceed to Carlisle Barracks in Pennsylvania, the site of the Medical Field Service School.

Clearly, it would not be long before I headed overseas.

The leatherbound clock that came at graduation time had started me thinking again about Aki. I had not seen her since November 1942, more than a year earlier. We had met briefly in Chicago for a visit when she was on her way from the assembly center at Santa Anita Racetrack in Arcadia, California, to join her sister in New York City. It had been a friendly but not romantic meeting—just old friends from UCLA with a lot of reminiscing to do.

As best I could recall my geography, New York was on the way from Chicago to Carlisle Barracks in Pennsylvania. So I wrote a short note. Could I see her en route to my new assignment?

Her schedule had some flexibility. She was a student then at Teachers College, Columbia University, working her way by serving as the secretary of International House near the university campus. Yes, she wrote back, we would be able to meet.

It was one of those marvelous reunions that somehow were enhanced by the compression of wartime. Our explorations of Manhattan even included a ride through Central Park in a horse-drawn carriage.

I was swept off my feet and proposed marriage. It was preposterous, I suppose. We had never been on a date; we were just casual friends from our university days in California. She had given me a box of special stationery at my going-away party at the rectory of St. Mary's Church in Los Angeles when I left for Marquette. We had exchanged a few letters. That was all. But, preposterous or not, I proposed.

"I guess I'll have to think about it, Jim," she replied. I took comfort from the fact that at least she did not say no, and I was certainly acting with a determination that contrasted with my father's decade-long wait to claim his bride.

As the days passed with no response, I became more and more anxious. One night, I told the officer in the next bunk about the marriage proposal I had made while in New York and of my frustration at not receiving an answer. Without hesitating, he dispatched me to the nearest telephone to call Aki.

Aki was astounded. She had written the answer in a letter mailed earlier that very day, she told me. And what was her answer? "*Hai!*" —yes, in Japanese.

In a state of excitement and exultation, I consulted the chaplain the next morning. What about a marriage license? Could I get a short leave? The answer came two days later, when our entire unit was drawn up in formation. I was ordered to step front and center. The officer of the day announced in crisp and commanding words that he was temporarily dismissing Lieutenant Yamazaki. The band struck up the wedding march, and there was a rousing cheer from my fellow medical officers.

We were married April 1, 1944, in Grace Episcopal Church on Broadway in New York City by my father and his friend the Reverend George Wieland. The *New York Times* carried a photograph with a brief caption: "Americans of Japanese descent wed here."

The next day we returned to Carlisle, Aki to the Molly Pitcher Hotel, I to the barracks. Our honeymoon came later, arranged by the United Service Organization (USO) at a farmhouse in the snow-covered Poconos, a brief interlude before I had to report to O'Reilley General Hospital in Springfield, Missouri.

On the way to Missouri we had a final Manhattan celebration that almost ended in disaster. I lost my wallet. Aki's resources were not quite equal to the bill brought by our waiter at the end of a festive night-club evening. A man at the next table seemed to sense our predicament. He insisted on paying our check and waved us on our way with a broad smile. We never learned his name.

Just before we were to leave Missouri for my next assignment, Aki awoke one morning with a fever and a rash. The symptoms seemed innocuous but proved otherwise. At the time, I thought it might be something associated with her pregnancy. It was not. It was German measles. We set aside our worries under the pressure to take up the next assignment, my last before going overseas. We would have been far more anxious had we known then what we know now about the possible consequences of German measles during pregnancy.

The invasion of France was under way when I reported for duty as surgeon of the 590th Field Artillery Battalion in the 106th Infantry Division at Camp Atterbury in Franklin, Indiana. The division was ready to ship out. Part of the group left almost immediately, to serve as urgently needed replacements for casualties as the war moved closer to Germany itself. New recruits flowed in, many of them green, with only limited training.

As the time for departure neared, there was a moment of embarrassment for me. One of the final formalities was a combat-readiness inspection. It was a test that included the medical units as well as the combat units. In the divisional critique, the inspecting general announced an irregularity in the medical unit: Lieutenant Yamazaki, he intoned, instead of saluting the visiting general, had extended his arm for a friendly handshake. The other officers guffawed.

Aki and I said goodbye at the beginning of November. Our generous landlord and landlady in Indiana used their precious gasoline ration to drive Aki to Cincinnati to await the birth of our baby. I sailed with the division from Boston. Six weeks later I would be in combat.

I sailed aboard the *Wakefield,* which crossed the Atlantic without escort because she was presumed fast enough to elude enemy submarines. The remainder of the division crossed on the *Queen Elizabeth* and the *Aquitania*. We docked at Liverpool without incident. But then events began to move with awesome speed. We had hardly reached our encampment in the Midlands when we were moved to Southampton to board landing craft for the Channel crossing.

I invaded the continent twice, as it turned out. Only two weeks after our arrival in Liverpool, we were in convoy to Le Havre aboard an LST (landing ship, tank), the largest of the invasion craft, a four-thousand ton vessel capable of transporting tanks and trucks as well as troops. But we had to return to England because Le Havre could not handle all of the ships that were arriving.

My second crossing was even more adventurous. In mid-Channel, in the middle of the night, I was ordered to transfer to another vessel to attend a critically ill seaman. I was lowered into the black water in a small skiff, and we made our way in darkness. Ahead I could dimly see a rope ladder trailing from a boom. "Jump for the ladder when the waves are just right," a voice called from above. Miraculously, I made it. The sailor had pneumonia, not the infected appendix suspected by the hospital corpsman, and he responded quickly to treatment.

I was able to arrange my first message home to Aki as we sipped coffee in the wardroom of that ship. An officer bound for rotation home after four years at sea offered to call her. He did. She was the first in the family to learn of my night sea adventure, and that I was with the fighting forces on the continent.

After getting ashore, I found my medical unit within the 106th Infantry Division, which was just setting out on a three-hundred-mile overland run to southeastern Belgium, to the Ardennes Forest—to the largest and costliest land battle of the war: the Battle of the Bulge. More than a million men were to be engaged in that battle.

The vast procession of vehicles and ten thousand men entered Belgium uneventfully. Eight days after arriving at Le Havre, we were in position in a forest maze of trees and hills. It had been quiet on that front since September. The Allied commanders were confident that the difficult terrain would discourage any German assault. A quiet front was appropriate for the inexperienced troops that made up most of our division.

Perhaps it was just that confidence that the German High Command counted on as they secretly massed troops for an enormous attack, a last desperate effort to break through the Allied front and turn back the conquest of Germany itself. They almost succeeded.

Aki could time the beginning of the battle. My letters stopped abruptly after December 15. Tranquility yielded to a terrifying bombardment on the sixth day in our position. It was December 16. By nightfall, our aid station in a farmhouse basement was crowded with wounded men, Germans among them, evidence of the depth of their infiltration. I was the only physician in the aid center, but I had the support of a team of enlisted men led by Sergeants George Bullard and George Pinna. We could offer little more than morphine to ease the pain of the wounded. They required evacuation, but we were cut off from the rear, and no ambulance could reach us.

The blazing warfare continued for two more days, although our medical unit did not come under direct fire. And the chaos increased. American units found themselves facing other American units, squeezed together by the German encirclement.

At night, we dug foxholes in the snow-covered ground and piled trees around them for protection from ricocheting bullets and shrapnel. We were in our foxhole one night when we heard approaching steps and the voices of a German patrol. Had they suspected we were there, a hand grenade would have finished us.

As dawn broke, disaster seemed imminent. We were sitting ducks. I could see the American trucks trapped, bumper to bumper, in the valley, surrounded by German units pouring intense fire on them.

Sergeant Pinna, a stretcher slung over his shoulder, started down the hillside toward the sound of battle, calling "Medic, medic," ready to help the wounded. I had no recollection of seeing him again, although many years later, when we reestablished contact, he said he had returned with a wounded soldier and I had amputated the soldier's foot. Such was the trauma of those moments that I did not remember the surgery. There is much that mercifully has been erased from my memory of that time.

In the midst of this desperate situation, I saw Major Irving Tietze, our executive officer, stand up in the face of enemy fire, a white cloth attached to a stick. We were surrendering.

German officers ordered our medical unit to continue treating the wounded. We filled twenty-eight trucks with casualties. All of our supplies were exhausted, and still the wounded came. What frustration. But it was nothing compared with the despair I felt a few minutes later when I was ordered to march out with the other prisoners of war.

I never learned the fate of the wounded men waiting in those twenty-eight trucks. At a veterans' reunion in 1991, a man who had been on the grave registration detail told me of being sent to the battle scene when the action was over and digging hundreds of bodies from the snow.

The Germans marched our ragged prisoner group away from the action. We moved past the remains of bodies dismembered in the ferocity of the fight. I was numb, unable to place myself in this scene of savagery, kept moving and alive by some primitive urge for survival. We were bedraggled and hungry, stricken with the fatigue of fear, sleep deprivation, and the tragedy of comrades lost in the struggle. We marched for fifty miles, finally coming to rest in what we later learned was Koblenz on the Rhine.

We were loaded into boxcars and began a strange pilgrimage, never quite sure where we were, catching glimpses through the slats in the sides of the boxcars. A great cathedral. Perhaps it was

Cologne, we speculated. Then another city, and the ominous sound of air raid sirens, followed by the approaching roar of bombers. The guards locked us in the boxcars and ran to nearby bomb shelters in the railyard of what must have been Hanover. There was a distant thud of the first bombs, then more, closer, until the boxcar vibrated and shook.[5]

I was taken from the train just before Christmas and placed in a prisoner-of-war camp at Falingbostel. A church service in the camp celebrated Christmas. It gave me a sense of continuity with the many Christmas services I had joined at St. Mary's, now empty of its Japanese-American congregation.

My only Christmas gift was a cup of coffee, the first and last I would have as a prisoner. It was presented by some French prisoners who had managed to save a few packets of instant Nescafé.

Our desperation was measured by the way we quarrelled over the division of rations. One day, the guards distributed a few special Christmas food boxes to us Americans but gave none to the Russian prisoners in the adjoining area. The Americans voted not to share. We were shamefaced a week later when Saint Nicholas Day boxes were distributed to the Russians and they promptly brought their boxes over to share with us.

Honest John had the hardest job among us. We had chosen him to slice the bread. He did it with remarkable fairness, but never without criticism, for every crumb counted in our hunger.

Three weeks after I arrived at the camp, on January 17, 1945, my family was informed that I was missing in action. But they did not have long to wait for assurance that I was alive. We were invited to broadcast messages. The transmission was monitored in the United States by ham operators, and thirty of them relayed cards to Aki that I was safe. One card, decorated with swastikas, asserted that I was being well treated, something of an exaggeration.

Despair and depression were constantly with us. There simply was no certainty of survival. We never knew what the next day would bring.

"I just want to tell you something," one of my fellow prisoners, an army captain, said one day. "The time may come when it's a question of you or me, and I want you to know that it's going to be me." I could only respect his honesty. He was never put to the test.

Our basic diet was a small ration of potatoes, which we cooked ourselves over a wood-burning stove. We supplemented potatoes by exchanging recollections of feasts from the past, of prized recipes. I still have a scrap of paper on which I wrote the recipe for bean, pork, and dumpling stew, the favorite of a second lieutenant from Georgia, who insisted that it always be served with cornbread and turnip greens.

One day an animal carcass was paraded through the camp. Meat? But the soup at the next meal seemed no different from the last. We never found anything solid in the weak broth.

We received gift packages once, distributed by Swiss relief workers. For many of the prisoners in our group, the cigarettes were the most welcome part of the packages. I lectured futilely on the importance of nutrition, but it did not slow the bartering of food for cigarettes. I chose the food and happily traded my cigarettes for an extra ration of powdered milk.

There was a succession of camps over the next five months as we followed a thousand-mile course circling south to Bavaria. Half the way we walked, half we covered in freight trains.

We spent two months at Offlag XIII-B at Hammelberg. It was a good vantage point from which to watch the war. We could see Frankfurt am Main in the distance as waves of Allied bombers attacked the city. Little did we know how near the American ground forces were. Then, suddenly, one afternoon, tanks of the Third Army roared up to the camp.

This armored group had penetrated fifty miles into German-held territory. We ran joyously out of the camp and gathered in a nearby forest for the night. At the first light of day, we started west. I tried riding on top of one of the American tanks, but the soldier driving it warned that it would be too dangerous because his was to be the lead tank, likely to draw the heaviest enemy fire. Captain James Fonda and I, both taken prisoner at the Battle of the Bulge, crowded aboard a half-track.

We had gone scarcely two miles when the column encountered German armored units. There was an explosion nearby. The tank I had tried to ride was hit. We could see the muzzles of guns on more German tanks moving toward us. We jumped to the ground and ran back into the woods.

Our liberation was short-lived. Twenty-four hours later, our rescuers had fallen into a German ambush and were forced to surrender. All eighteen of the armored vehicles in that group were destroyed, and the men were killed or captured. We were rounded up in the forest where we had taken cover and returned to the prisoner-of-war camp.

There were reports that the risky venture had been ordered to rescue Colonel John K. Waters, the son-in-law of General George Patton, Third Army commander. Waters was wounded in the unsuccessful attempt. I could only question the wisdom of such a venture.

Soon we were on the move again—weeks and more weeks of marching and waiting, hunger compounding our weariness. I narrowly escaped being caught in the Allied bombing of Nuremberg, which began just as we were being marched out of the city. Our column of prisoners stretched more than two miles. Those of us at the front of the column were spared. Many of those at the rear, including my friend Lieutenant John Lott, who had been captured with me in the Ardennes, were killed by the American bombs.

More than once we were subjected to strafing by American fighter planes that mistook us for marching German troops. I can still vividly hear and feel that experience, seeking shelter in a ditch by the road, looking up to see the American planes just above us as bullets shattered the trees and ground around us. In the terror of those attacks, I doubted that I would ever get home.

There was not much to laugh at during those grueling weeks, but I do recall one amusing encounter. I found myself in one camp facing a Soviet soldier of Asian extraction. He was equally surprised at seeing me, an American soldier of Asian extraction. We spoke, using our limited German vocabularies. He told me he was from Mongolia. I explained my family's origins in Japan.

"You went to a lot of trouble to get here," he commented.

"Well, you came a long way, too," I replied. And we actually laughed together at our misadventures.

We were losing so much weight that we had to hold up our trousers. One colleague who found a weighing scale reported that he had lost sixty-five pounds. Our misery was compounded by lice. There was the constant itching, the ineffective scratching. Once, we were issued razors and told to shave our bodies in a futile effort to control the lice. We stood in the snow to do it. It didn't help. That was the only time we were permitted to shave in the five-month period. Fortunately, there was little skin disease even though we had been allowed only one shower.

I do recall one pleasant occasion. One of our guards, with whom I had struck up some conversations, arranged for the sick prisoners who were under my care to spend several days at a small farm. The farmer and his wife shared their fresh-baked bread, soup—real soup—and vegetables with us. And a German medical officer was able to get me a supply of a special tannic acid preparation that helped some of the men with serious intestinal problems. Other than that, I had nothing with which to treat injuries or illness.

In our final wearisome trek we covered 150 miles, most of it on foot, over the winding back roads of Bavaria. At long last we reached our destination: Mooseberg.

Incredible. I could hardly believe my first impressions. It was so similar in so many ways to Camp Jerome, the detention camp in Arkansas where American authorities had incarcerated my parents and sister. There were the same guard towers, the same floodlights, the same barbed wire, the same heavily armed military guard. I had been but a temporary and voluntary guest visiting my family at Camp Jerome. Here I was a prisoner of America's enemy.

Mooseberg lies northeast of Munich. At that time it probably was the largest prisoner-of-war camp operated by the Germans. I was one of seventy thousand prisoners, including soldiers not only from the United States and its European allies but also from Nigeria and India. The Sikhs from India set an example for all of us with their neatness, alongside our bedraggled appearance, and their spirited morale.

I was appointed the camp's sanitation officer, an assignment that allowed me to move freely around the camp to check the sorry state of the latrines and also to visit with the diverse prisoner population. I encountered some Japanese-American veterans of the celebrated 100th/442d Regimental Combat Team and learned from them of the battlefield deaths of two old friends from St. Mary's in Los Angeles.

It was at Mooseberg that I was liberated for the second time, again by the Third Army, but on this occasion the liberation was permanent. General Patton's troops freed us at the end of April as they swept south and east. I learned that I was no longer a prisoner when a loaf of white bread unexpectedly arrived in our unit. We had seen nothing like it since our capture. The Third Army had dropped off food for us even as it sped east to complete the liberation of Germany.

With the prison camp gates no longer locked, we were free to explore the region. But we were warned not to be gone long lest we miss the train that would take us to a port of embarkation. Confusion outweighed elation, perhaps because of our utter weariness. We had no way of knowing how close to victory the Allies were. But I enjoyed at least the end of confinement and the relaxed feeling of strolling through the nearby towns.

Our evacuation train had just pulled into the station at Rheims when we were told that the Germans had surrendered unconditionally. That was May 7. The official proclamation came the next day in Berlin. The war in Europe was over.

We were more interested in getting home than in celebrating. I recall our impatience in the weeks at Camp Lucky Strike at Le Havre waiting for a place on one of the transports sailing back to the United States. My turn came at the end of May. I was named ship's surgeon for a vessel full of returning former prisoners of war. The biggest problem was to see that they did not over-eat after months of near starvation.

The welcome in New York was enormous. The harbor was filled with fireboats spraying columns of water and other ships and boats blasting their whistles. From crowded ferryboats, young women threw kisses and bands played. Someone tried to get us to sing, but none of us felt like singing just then.

Red Cross and USO women met us on the dock with banks of telephones at their disposal. I wasn't sure where Aki might be, but the staff on the dock quickly traced her to the home of her sister in nearby Mamaroneck. By chance, she answered the phone herself.

"I'm home," I said, almost speechless at hearing her voice. She had had no way of knowing when I would return. We planned an immediate reunion. After seven months that seemed like seven years, I would see Aki again and meet the baby she was bearing when I left. Was it a boy or a girl?

5 HOMECOMING AND THE BOMB

The reunion in Mamaroneck was bittersweet.

Aki met me at the door with a wonderful, warm, welcoming embrace.

"How is the baby?" I blurted out in my excitement. With tears in her eyes, Aki told me the sad news. Noel James had been born with a malformed heart. He had died shortly after birth, a son I would never know. It must have been the German measles. In later years, that tragedy would inspire my deep concern about malformations, part of the study we would make in Nagasaki and Hiroshima.

For the moment, we had no place of our own to stay. Aki had tried to rent an apartment, running want ads that said "returning G.I.—Prisoner of War needs apartment." There were responses, but when she went in person to work out the lease, she was invariably turned away.

New York even then had a reputation for being cosmopolitan, hospitable, the melting pot of the world. But there was no room for returning Japanese-American veterans. And, to add to the insult, a stranger approached us one day as we walked in the city, I in my uniform, and said: "Why don't you go back to where you came from?"

We used up my accumulated back pay staying in hotels. But we also managed family reunions—with my parents in Chicago, and with my brother Peter, then in special training at Fort Snelling near Minneapolis. And the army provided a memorable rest and recre-

ation stay at the sumptuous Grove Park Inn in Asheville, North
Carolina, in August.

While we were in Asheville, the local newspaper reported one
morning the introduction of a new weapon in the war against Japan.
A super bomb. We paid only passing attention. An "atomic bomb"
meant nothing to us. We were caught up in the joy of being reunited
and planning our future life together. Even the news of a second
bomb, this one dropped on Nagasaki, seemed unimportant.

Only in subsequent days, when the newspaper speculated that
Japan's surrender was at hand, did we begin to appreciate the importance of the weapon. But its devastation in human terms was not
then apparent. Nor could we have guessed how central to our lives
the survivors of those bombs would become.

Celebration of the victory against Japan was subdued. For reasons
I shall never understand, all of us at the Grove Park Inn were con-
fined to quarters on V-J Day. And the bar at the inn itself was ordered
closed by the military officials running the rest and rehabilitation
program.

We welcomed, of course, the recreation. But we could not conceal our surprise regarding some elements of the program. We were,
for example, required to attend lectures on the meaning of democ-
racy and "What are we fighting for?" I cannot imagine an audience
that needed that sort of information less than this group of battle
veterans.

My transition to civilian life was greatly helped by my final six-
month military assignment as a ward officer at Lovell General Hospital near Leominster, Massachusetts. I developed a close camara-
derie with my patients, casualties of combat from the Pacific and
European theaters. But even as I worked among the veterans, I was
determined to proceed to pediatric training.

Aki made it possible by agreeing to support us during the long
training period, supplementing the education funds available to all

veterans under the G.I. Bill. While we were at Lovell, she helped me complete almost a hundred applications for medical residencies. Thousands of doctors whose training had been interrupted by military service were doing the same thing.

The medical staff at Lovell Hospital included a professor from the University of Pennsylvania Medical School completing his military service. His support helped me win appointment to the university's Children's Hospital in Philadelphia and its strong teaching program under the direction of Dr. Joseph Stokes, Jr.

My fifteen months at Children's Hospital were influential in developing my understanding of the interrelationship of health and social factors. The hospital, at 1740 Bainbridge Street, was the oldest pediatric hospital in the nation. It was surrounded by a neighborhood of low-income African-American families.

My training included the opportunity to work closely with some of those families, and I grew to appreciate even more the importance of understanding the family situation in order to treat the child effectively. I still marvel at the generosity of several of those women. When they found abandoned babies on their doorsteps, they welcomed the infants as members of their families, even though they already were living in poverty and were unsure they could feed their own children.

This was also a period of strong emphasis on the importance of preventive medicine. Doctors were learning more about the stages of illness, which helped us to respond better to sick children. Surgery for children was then being developed by a young faculty member, C. Everett "Chick" Koop, who would become celebrated as the independent-minded and conscientious surgeon general of the 1980s who forced a reluctant President Ronald Reagan to become engaged in the devastating AIDS pandemic.

Aki was working at the American Friends Service Committee as secretary to Professor Gilbert White, later the president of Haverford

College. It was a friendship that flowered during those months that inspired this book. Aki's fellow student at Columbia, Cola Franzen, was working in the same office while her husband, Wolfgang, was working on his Ph.D. in physics. Forty-three years later, they would urge me to write this memoir.

I completed my residency at the Children's Hospital of Cincinnati, where, in 1947, I had the good fortune to be accepted for a two-year pediatric program. It was to prove crucial in my later involvement with the children of Nagasaki.

The move was important to me because the Cincinnati program offered two services that I could not get in Philadelphia: working with newborns and with infectious diseases at the neighboring Cincinnati General Hospital.

I had two particular mentors among the many outstanding teachers at Cincinnati. One was Dr. Ashley A. Weech, who was in charge of my program. He was more than a great teacher. He also arranged housing for Aki and me when we were turned away from apartment after apartment because of our Japanese ancestry. The other was Dr. Katharine Dodd, whose demand for absolutely full attention to each case became the standard for my care of every patient during my career as a pediatrician. We named our first daughter for her.

Medicine was still far removed at that time from the levels of care and cure now available. Dr. Dodd was just beginning to treat tuberculosis with streptomycin, one of the miracle drugs that would reverse the ravages of tuberculosis, making it a treatable disease instead of a source of terror and death. Dr. Albert Sabin was at work then at the same hospital developing an oral vaccine for the prevention of poliomyelitis. We residents were treating two buildings full of polio patients in respirators, a stark reminder of how much a vaccine was needed.

Dr. George Lyons, a pediatric cardiologist, was developing well-baby clinics, opening my eyes still wider to the desperate need for preventive care for poor families in the inner city. Dr. Fred Silverman, who was working to focus national attention on the horrors of child abuse, shared with us his pioneering work with X rays to identify fracture evidence of abuse.

The meeting that would focus my career on the children of the atomic bombs came in January 1948. Dr. Weech, the head of our training program, had just returned from a meeting in Washington called by the National Research Council of the National Academy of Sciences. Unknown to most of us, a presidential order to the National Research Council had established the Committee on Atomic Casualties in 1947. The committee in turn had decided to set up the Atomic Bomb Casualty Commission (ABCC) to undertake a long-term study. Two months later, I had a meeting with Dr. Weech, who urged me to go to work for the commission.

A major element of the commission's work would be to study the effects of the atomic bombs on the children of Hiroshima and Nagasaki, he told me.[6] Before I could respond, he digressed for a moment. He recalled how he, as a young faculty member at Johns Hopkins Medical School, had gone to teach at Peking Union Medical College. The experience of living in China, a very different culture far from home, had changed his entire outlook on people, and medicine. It had been a rich and rewarding experience. "Furthermore," he continued, "you'll be entering on the ground floor of a new era of atomic medicine. Think about it, Jim. Talk it over with Aki."

Aki and I were both skeptical at first. We had shared a dream of completing the pediatric training and returning to Los Angeles to open a private practice there. I agreed, nevertheless, to attend briefings in Washington by scientists of the Committee on Atomic Casualties. The scope of the study was still being developed when I had my first interviews, and it was clear that participants would have an opportunity to submit their personal preferences regarding the research.

Much work had already been done regarding the short-term effects of the two bombs. Immediately after the bombings, Japanese doctors conducted a survey of the survivors. Two months later, a joint commission of Japanese and American physicians made an exhaustive medical survey of the bomb's effects. It was this report and its findings of massive casualties and unbelievable destruction that had prompted the surgeon general to call for research on the other effects, with a special emphasis on the effects on children. Little was then known about the long-term effects of entire body irradiation, or about the genetic consequences.

Dr. Weech suggested that I should focus, if I took the job, on two areas: the effects on growth and development of the survivors, and the incidence of malformations. Was there impairment of growth? Could specific disorders be traced to the massive exposure to radiation? Did the exposure of the embryo in pregnant women in the two cities result in malformation or elevated rates of miscarriage?

My interest grew quickly, for this was a new field of study, a virtually unexplored subject, and the death of my son had awakened a concern about the paucity of medical knowledge about malformations. We knew almost nothing. But studies of incidental or accidental exposure to other forms of radiation had indicated the likelihood that the risks were enormous to all exposed to massive radiation.

Some of that early work on malformation was being done at the Cincinnati Children's Hospital Research Institute at that very time by Dr. Joseph Warkany, who eventually came to be acknowledged worldwide as a leader in teratology, the study of malformations. Dr. Warkany was able to elaborate on earlier findings concerning malformations among children born to mothers who had been exposed to high doses of X rays. His research led us to watch for reduced head size and mental retardation among the Nagasaki and Hiroshima survivors.

An agreement was negotiated permitting me to work with Dr. Warkany, squeezing in these studies on top of my regular residency requirements. It was intense, but very stimulating. Step by step I was being drawn deeper and deeper into the study of the problems of radiation — and toward Hiroshima and Nagasaki.

My final decision to go to work for the Atomic Bomb Casualty Commission came in September 1948 after I was assured of Dr. Warkany's help. That decision in turn led me, early in 1949, to the office of Dr. James Neel, a medical geneticist at the University of Michigan at Ann Arbor.

Dr. Neel had initiated the study of babies conceived after the bombs were dropped on Nagasaki and Hiroshima. Were there genetic defects in these children? One aspect of this study would be the search for malformations. Babies in the womb at the time of the bombings, babies conceived after the bombings, and young children in the bombed cities would be included in the study. Pediatricians were needed.

Aki and I knew, when we decided to go to Japan, that we would take our newborn son, Paul, with us. But we faced a dilemma. How could we protect him from the tuberculosis then rampant in Japan? I finally decided that we had no choice but to administer the live tuberculosis bacteria vaccine then available.

No one at Cincinnati Children's Hospital had experience with the vaccine, let alone in calculating the appropriate dosage for a four-month-old baby. We knew there was a remote chance that the vaccine could infect him rather than protect him. Perhaps we were more apprehensive because of the death of our firstborn. Not until much later did we know that we had done the correct thing. He escaped tuberculosis.

The vaccine adventure was but a small part of the seemingly endless formalities of the year of preparing for our departure. Among other things, we had to obtain special permission from the Supreme Commander of the Allied Powers in Tokyo to waive the rule against allowing babies into countries under occupation.

As the day for leaving approached, we were assured that all was in order, including housing for the three of us when we reached Hiroshima. It was the first of many false assurances, the first of many uncertainties and disappointments that accompanied our move.

We set out from Cincinnati in our first car, the cheapest Chevrolet on the market, with a pistachio green paint job that Aki and I will never forget. Our motor trip was arranged on a schedule that would allow time for a reunion with my family, who had been allowed to return to their home in Los Angeles at the end of the war with Japan.

The Committee on Atomic Casualties also instructed me to visit the dean of the new medical school at UCLA, Dr. Stafford Warren. All I knew then was that Dr. Warren had been among the first American physicians to visit both Hiroshima and Nagasaki after the bombs. Only later did I learn that he had been responsible for radiation safety for the entire Manhattan Project, which had developed those first bombs. He had also been a witness at the dawn of the atomic age when the world's first atomic blast lit the skies at Alamogordo, New Mexico, on July 16, 1945 — less than a month before the bombs were deployed against Japan.

Dr. Warren was friendly but, I suppose, under considerable restraint as to what he could share because of the secrecy still surrounding the bomb's human toll. There were no texts, no reports, no guidelines, he said. Ours was to be research into the unknown as we tried to understand the effects of exposure to the bombs' radiation. He told me only a little of what he had seen on that first inspection shortly after the bombings.

Just before I left, he offered a word of caution about personal security. He had been apprehensive on the first night of his visit to Hiroshima, understanding the anger of the people toward the United States. So he slept that night with his service revolver at his side.

In fact, he had had no problems. The Japanese physicians worked in close cooperation with their American counterparts to make a thorough study of more than thirteen thousand survivors, gathering important evidence on the short-term effects. Unfortunately, the findings of this joint study were not made available to me until 1956.

Now, Dr. Warren was saying to me, the critical test will be whether we can discern effects that were not apparent in those first examinations immediately after the bombing.

Thus the stage was set for the two great thrusts of research: the effects of the radiation on survivors, and the impact of the bombs in terms of genetic damage.

Aki, with five-month-old Paul in her arms, stood beside me at the rail of the *President Cleveland,* staring west, until finally we could make out the silhouette of land — Japan. We had at last reached the land of our ancestors.

My feelings were mixed. I was excited at the prospect of seeing Japan, of being involved in the groundbreaking research on the effects of the atomic bombs. But I felt the uncertainty of being less than fluent in the language, of knowing none of the officials with whom I would be working, of being truly American, not Japanese, a stranger in the land of my roots. I did not know at that moment how justified my feeling of uncertainty would prove to be.

I could not help recalling, as we approached Yokohama, the misadventure of my father's departure forty-five years before. As a tugboat pulled his ship away from the dock, perhaps the same pier we were approaching, he untied the *furoshiki* that held his personal possessions, planning to wave it to friends on the dock below. The wind caught the cloth and sent the contents, including my father's trans-Pacific ticket, flying into the harbor. He had to purchase a duplicate and wait a year for a refund.

As our ship eased against the pier in Yokohama, our spirits rose. There stood my brother Peter and his wife, Joy. After his service in the army occupation forces he had returned to Tokyo to continue service as a civilian employee of the U.S. government. Standing on the pier with him were several lifelong friends from Los Angeles.

Special passport issued to James, Aki, and Paul Yamazaki in 1949 for travel to Japan on official business.

They were among the thousands of Japanese Americans who had been trained in the Military Intelligence Service Language School and now were playing a crucial role working for the supreme commander of the Allied powers overseeing the occupation.

No sooner had we exchanged greetings with Peter and our old friends, however, than our enthusiasm was dampened. An administrator from the Atomic Bomb Casualty Commission offered official greetings and then informed us that the promised housing was not available. Aki and Paul must remain in Tokyo while I proceeded alone to Hiroshima. I was furious. But what could I do? And I was eager to get on with the work.

Dr. Warren had asked me to call on Dr. Masao Tsuzuki at Tokyo Imperial University to extend his personal good wishes. I had no idea who this man might be. And I was concerned that my Japanese would be inadequate. But I persevered, and we had a warm and friendly meeting. By some miracle, the university had been spared in the extensive bombing of Tokyo, which included firebombings that killed an estimated 88,000 people.

This visit could have been of extraordinary help to me in the work

I was about to undertake had I known Dr. Tsuzuki's background.[7] I suppose it was concern about security that had discouraged Dr. Warren from providing that information. I did not know that it was Dr. Tsuzuki who had mobilized an immediate research program by Japanese doctors working with the survivors of the atomic bomb attacks. I did not see the excellent report of the Japanese doctors until I returned to Japan in 1989.[8]

Nor did I know that it was Dr. Tsuzuki who, with Dr. Warren, had directed the vast study of the short-term effects of the bomb radiation undertaken by American and Japanese specialists just two months after the bombs fell. The work of the Joint Commission for the Study of the Effects of the Atomic Bomb in Japan had been a great success, bringing together physicians of the conquering and defeated nations bound by a common concern for the thousands of victims.

Dr. Tsuzuki's role had been pivotal, for he could muster support based on his influence as a nationally celebrated professor of surgery at Tokyo University as well as his exalted rank as an admiral in the medical arm of the Japanese Navy during the war. It was this Joint Commission's report that I did not see until 1956. I did not even know it existed when I met with Dr. Tsuzuki.

During our brief stay in Tokyo, Aki and I were able for the first time to meet cousins and other family members, who dropped in at Peter's house for informal family reunions. In the forty-five years since my father's emigration, only one relative from Japan, one of my mother's brothers, had visited us in Los Angeles. How ironic that it should take a war to bring us together.

Aki and Paul moved into the already crowded quarters shared by Peter and his wife, Joy, in "Washington Heights," the housing project adjacent to Meiji Park for American occupation workers. Had Peter not been there, my family would have been homeless. Still angry at the broken promise concerning housing, I left for Hiroshima.

There were very few signs of the war that had ended scarcely four years earlier. In Yokohama and Tokyo and along the rail line to Hiroshima there was an appearance of normality. And when I arrived at my destination, I was isolated from the worst of the damage. I left the train at Kure, thirty miles east of the center of Hiroshima. All the occupation forces were quartered in and around Kure. And my work with the ABCC was centered in Ujina, the port section of the city of Hiroshima, about six miles from the hypocenter. I was caught up in such a heavy work schedule that I did not have an opportunity at that time to visit the bombed-out center of the city. My first view of the reality of atomic destruction did not come until two months later, when I was in Nagasaki.

I had a hint of things to come on my first evening in Kure. I was walking down the street with a colleague when a passing group of Australian soldiers shoved me roughly to the side. My colleague tried to calm me, saying that this sort of action was commonplace in that area, which was administered by the British Commonwealth Occupation Forces. Some of the soldiers were utterly insensitive to the civilian population. I realized that they could not distinguish between a Japanese and a Japanese American. But I found their behavior an awful indictment of the arrogance they brought to the occupation.

The next day, I opened the question of housing. Alas, I was told, it would not be easy. The American housing compound, where I would have been welcome, was full. And the British housing compound, which had numerous vacancies, barred civilians, including Americans, "of Japanese extraction" under a policy that had been approved by the Supreme Command in Tokyo.[9] I was not to worry, however. Housing would be found, I was assured, but no one said when. The last place I had expected to be discriminated against was in occupied Japan.

As I waited a month for a house, seething over the British occupation policy, I often recalled the record of the Japanese Americans in combat and on secret intelligence missions behind Japanese lines. "The Nisei saved countless Allied lives and shortened the war by two years," General Charles Willoughby, G-2 intelligence chief on General MacArthur's staff, had said.

Soon we were given a house in nearby Aga. But we were not allowed to use the local service bus operated by the British forces for the families of the occupation units. The British school, the only one in the area that offered instruction in English, also was closed to American civilians of Japanese extraction. This did not affect Paul, who was much too young for school, but it forced a Japanese-American colleague and his wife to teach their daughter at home. Furthermore, the isolated location of our house outside the normal compound area raised security questions. It was agreed that a special guard would be provided.

I suppose my concern about security was based in part on a frightening experience I had had as a prisoner of war in Germany. Our column of prisoners had been making its way near a town that had suffered severe damage from Allied aerial bombing. On seeing us, the angry villagers gathered, threatening to attack our group, their particular rage aimed against the airmen, identifiable by their leather flight jackets. Only the intervention of German troops rescued us from their attack. And I also had in mind Dr. Warren's recollection of spending his first night in Hiroshima with a revolver at his side.

As my work in Japan unfolded, there were never any security problems. The precautions apparently were not necessary.

My protest about the discrimination against Americans of Japanese descent by the British occupation forces reverberated. I was interviewed by Carl Mydans of *Life* magazine and Keyes Beech of the *Chicago Daily News,* and I learned later that the wire services also carried stories about the racist British policies. The publicity did not help me. It only aggravated the administrators, one of whom simply suggested that I might just as well pack up and go back to the United States.

Matters were very different within the community of physicians and other scientists gathering for the important monitoring work. I found myself quickly engaged in projects with Dr. Wataru Sutow, a Stanford-trained pediatrician who was in charge of pediatrics; Dr. Wayne Borges, a hematologist; and his wife, Dr. Jane Borges, a pediatrician, who had come from Children's Hospital in Boston. They encouraged my interest in studying the effects of bomb radiation exposure on fetuses.

In the days that followed, I established a close working relationship with all of the specialists. These relationships proved invaluable when I later found myself in Nagasaki.

Aki could share the warmth and hospitality of my new colleagues only in the evening. During the day she lived in exile in our remote house. Under the Australian-British occupation rules, she could not even visit the commissary with the other wives. It was out of bounds to those of Asian extraction.

As a matter of fact, much of the social life was also out of bounds to us. Invitations were placed in all of the pigeonhole mailboxes, including mine, whenever there was to be a major party. But the invitations from the British and Australian units invariably included a proviso that the invitation was for those "of European descent only."

No sooner had we settled in for the two-year assignment than another surprise came. The director of the program summoned me for a meeting. I was being dispatched to Nagasaki to serve, alone, with no American medical colleagues, as physician in charge of the work of the ABCC there. I suspected then, and I remain suspicious today, that the new assignment was a punishment for objecting to the housing rules and racial restrictions.

Had I known then what a rewarding experience Nagasaki would provide, I would not have resisted. But I was shocked. I had been recruited as a pediatrician and had looked forward to clinical work with the bomb survivors. I was impatient to get into the actual research, to get beyond planning. Instead, I was being converted into an administrator. I had a specific assignment when I left the United States. Now I was being ordered around as if I were still in the army. There was no one to hear my appeal, however. I had no recourse. Within days, I was aboard a train, bound for Nagasaki to survey the situation and, again, to struggle with the problem of housing.

Part of my hesitancy over the new job had to do with the fact that I would be starting almost from scratch. The commission had opened its study in Nagasaki a year earlier. The people who had begun the research were scattered around the city, with the main office over a fish market on a wharf. Dr. Robert Kurata, an American citizen trained at Keio University Medical School in Tokyo, had directed activities in the first year but was leaving. There were no laboratories, no clinics, no facilities for even preliminary examination of the survivors. I would be the only American doctor on the scene.

So that first trip to Nagasaki in November 1949 was solely to tie down some of the basic logistical elements, above all to find a building where we could consolidate our operations and create a clinic to begin examining the survivors. I could not imagine then that it would take more than a year to get the research program fully operational. I was accompanied by Dr. Grant Taylor, a professor of pediatrics at Duke University on loan as deputy director of the ABCC in Hiroshima.

We focused on the Kaikan Building. It was two and a half miles from the hypocenter, and surrounded by mountains and hills which had provided protection from most of the bomb's force. Before the bomb, the Kaikan Building had served as the Prefectural Teachers' Association headquarters. The U.S. military government had made use of it when the occupation began but now was moving all of its administrative offices in that part of Japan to nearby Sasebo. The Kaikan was ours for the asking.

We must have looked more like architects than pediatricians as we roamed the Kaikan, blueprints in hand, for two weeks, trying to devise a workable floorplan that would turn the building into the ABCC headquarters in Nagasaki. As pediatricians we were especially concerned about facilitating the movement of children and their mothers and grandmothers in anticipation of the clinical examinations that would be a central part of the research. Fortunately, Dr. Taylor had been an engineer before he took up medicine. We needed every bit of that engineering knowledge as we developed the extensive remodeling plan.

Our move from Hiroshima to Nagasaki was delayed until January because it was impossible to arrange a move during the New Year celebrations. New Year is the principal holiday of the year for the Japanese. In that troubled postwar period the people were particularly intent on observing a time of rest, religious ceremonies, family reunions, and special feasts, to the extent that continuing food scarcities would allow.

Sharing those Christmas and New Year celebrations with our new friends in Hiroshima was of special meaning to Aki and me. It was not easy anticipating my role as a lone operator in Nagasaki. I took every opportunity, in my final weeks in Hiroshima, to enjoy the professional satisfaction of sharing ideas and research goals with the remarkable team of gynecologists, hematologists, internists, radiologists, surgeons, and pediatricians that had been assembled.

The move came none too soon for me. Despite my anxiety about being on my own in Nagasaki, I was eager to get to work and frustrated by the delays that had kept me from beginning my pediatric research. I was disappointed that administrative responsibilities had been heaped on me, reducing my research opportunities. But I felt the challenge of the work and the need to move ahead in trying to grasp the effects of the bomb.

At least I would be close to some of the children of the bombs.

Four years and five months after the atomic bomb was dropped on Nagasaki, Aki, Paul, and I arrived to begin my work with the survivors. At this point only fragmentary data relating to the bomb's delayed effects had been published.

I was particularly anxious to launch my research on the impact of the bomb on the human fetus. There was also a need to strengthen the programs already under way, notably the study of genetic effects, of what succeeding generations could face.

Alas, more delays were in store for me. The remodeling of the Kaikan Building had been temporarily shelved while differences among agencies in Washington were resolved. The construction work would take several months, which meant a long wait before we could initiate full clinical research.

I later came to realize that there was a positive side to the delays. We still had a great deal to do to gain the confidence of the community. First of all, we needed the cooperation of the medical profession. And we had to win the confidence and cooperation of the parents of the children placed at risk by the bomb.

Out of the confusion and through the delay there emerged at last a most welcome decision from Washington. Children were to be the focus of our study in Nagasaki. I could not have been more pleased.

The local doctors who had themselves survived the bomb were quick to support our work and to join the research, despite the enormous personal tragedies they had suffered and the almost total destruction of the University Medical Center.[10] When the decision was made to make children the focus of our research, the University Medical Center offered its full cooperation. Within the year, the faculty elected Noriuki Izumi, chairman of the pediatrics department, as dean to facilitate this cooperation. In addition, the medical school gave its assurance of full academic standing at the university for staff doctors who spent a substantial amount of time away from the medical school helping our ABCC teams.

Atsuyoshi Takao and Masahiko Setoguchi are sterling examples of the quality of that cooperation. They came to us as young pediatricians and gave hours and hours to the work of the ABCC. Takao went on to study advanced pediatric cardiology in New York and Houston before returning to found the Japan Heart Institute at the Women's Medical College in Yokohama. Setoguchi, who continued in a pediatric practice in Nagasaki, made history with the first report on the bomb's impact on children to the Japan Pediatric Society.

The hypocenter was just east of the Urakami River, precisely halfway between the Mitsubishi-Urakami Ordnance and Torpedo Works, a mile to the north, and the Mitsubishi Steel and Arms Works, a mile to the south. It could not have been better targeted to destroy the heart of that important military-industrial complex.

But even closer to the point of detonation lay the Nagasaki University Medical School, scarcely a quarter mile away to the east, and the University Hospital, four-tenths of a mile to the southeast.

Dr. Raisuke Shirabe was at the hospital that cataclysmic August morning. When I first met Dr. Shirabe, he was seated beside the dean of the Nagasaki University Medical School. I had gone to that meeting with some trepidation, for I knew that the success of our work would depend largely on the cooperation of the faculty of this great institution. And I was again uncomfortable about my Japanese language skills.

I asked our staff interpreter to accompany me to make sure that I did not miss any nuances or create any confusion. To my surprise, the conversation proceeded smoothly. Only a few interventions by the interpreter were necessary. The doctors, in their eagerness to help, more than compensated for my deficiencies, quickly volunteering words whenever I paused.

One happy outcome of that introductory meeting was the appointment of Dr. Shirabe as liaison with our ABCC staff. As such, he opened the doors of the city for us, won extraordinary cooperation from the medical profession, and led me to other physicians whose stories broadened my understanding and helped in our interpretations of the reports on the children of Nagasaki. He was taller than most Japanese, with the darker skin characteristic of this southern region of Kyushu. I was most struck by his eyes, set deep in a face that crinkled engagingly when he smiled or laughed. His geniality concealed the trauma of his bomb experience, the tragedy of his family.

Dr. Shirabe, director of the University Hospital, had been at the hospital when the bomb detonated. He explained this quietly to me as we walked through the buildings where litter was still piled on the floor four years after the bombing.

He picked up a mass of glass, explaining that it was comprised of microscope slides fused by the bomb. Students sitting at that long lab table had died instantly, with no evidence of injury or burn. They were found slumped over their work.

"That's where the school and laboratories were," Dr. Shirabe said, pointing out the window. "They were constructed of wood." Nothing remained. In those structures, only three-tenths of a mile from the hypocenter, everyone died.

At eleven o'clock that August morning, hearing a plane, Dr. Shirabe had started to leave his office in the hospital surgery department for the air raid shelter.

"Just as I reached the doorway to the office, a silvery purple light

"As close as you can get to an atomic blast and still survive." The Nagasaki University Hospital viewed from the lower slopes of Mt. Kompira. There were scarcely any survivors in the adjacent Sakamoto district half a mile from the hypocenter. The concrete walls of the hospital absorbed some of the energy of the bomb, so more than half the occupants were able to survive. Courtesy of the Nagasaki University Medical School.

flashed from the window on the northern side of the room, followed immediately by a thunderous roar as the building shuddered and the walls and ceiling crashed around me. Fortunately the debris on my back was light enough to allow me to struggle to my feet. I opened my eyes and it was pitch black and completely silent."

He paused, then added, "I cannot describe in words the feeling at that moment of suddenly being utterly separated from the world that I knew."

Pandemonium broke the silence, he recalled. Terrorized patients and staff clambered out windows and doors, fleeing the hospital, fleeing the inferno that was consuming the city beyond the hospital buildings. Unable to reenter the building, he joined the mass of survivors making their way to the hills. Late in the afternoon, he returned with another doctor to the medical school campus, calling the name of his younger son, Koji. But there was no answer.

That night he slept under the stars, returning early the next day to help organize emergency relief centers for the refugees in a school and temple. Only when that work was done did he feel free to make his way home, several miles to the north in a neighborhood where only limited damage had occurred.

He was given a joyous welcome by his wife, four of his five children, and his eighty-year-old mother. No one in the family had known whether he had survived. His son Seichi, eighteen, lay swathed in bandages, critically burned when the bomb caught him at work at the Ohashi Ordnance Factory at the north end of the industrial area. And Koji, sixteen, for whom Shirabe had searched the afternoon before, had not come home from his classes as a first-year medical student. At least the family had some shelter. Only the roof and windows of their home north of the Urakami Valley had been damaged.

On the seventh day after the bomb, Seichi's "cries to his mother turned to a whisper," Dr. Shirabe wrote in his journal. "His discomfort cannot be relieved." Seichi died. "I obtained the assistance of several neighbors in carrying his body to a nearby hill for cremation. After the cremation, I went immediately to the relief stations to treat the patients."

Three weeks later, there was still no word about Koji.

"So with my wife and daughters we returned to the medical college to look for some clue of my son's fate." They found the clue in the rubble of a lecture hall: a shred of the blue serge trousers Koji had been wearing. There could be no doubt. The name of his cousin, who had given him the trousers, was neatly penned on the white lining. The body had been incinerated in the blast. Only a few bones, stacked in the center of the room, remained of those who had been studying there.

Dr. Shirabe himself fell victim to radiation illness and thought he would soon die. Many around him with the same symptoms did die, but he was among the fortunate ones. He recovered.

It was Dr. Shirabe who arranged an extraordinary briefing for me by hospital staff members who had survived the bomb. I realized how important this would be, for few survivors had been as close to the hypocenter as these fifteen doctors, nurses, and support staff personnel. I invited ABCC physicians from the commission headquarters in Hiroshima to join us.

We met in a small classroom in the shattered hospital, where reconstruction was just beginning. Dr. Shirabe assumed the role of professor and moderator, with carefully prepared charts and maps to help the visitors understand what had happened. Here he was, a man who had suffered incredibly in a personal and professional way, standing with pointer in hand as if he were lecturing on remote and impersonal events.

After the bomb was detonated over Nagasaki, Dr. Kohei Koyano, a professor of surgery, escaped the hospital by crawling out a window. The doors had been blocked by debris.

"I looked around and saw a huge brown cloud hanging over the sky and the sun looking bloody red through that cloud," he told us. "All around there were many students and nurses gathered, all suffering from wounds and in some the entire body was burned with skin hanging from their limbs and body like thin strips of paper, dipped in blood. They were in pain, thirsty, crying for water."

Doctors told of the cries of the patients as fire spread inside the hospital. One doctor was able to carry a patient out with him despite his own wounds. The nearby medical school was engulfed in flames. A massive exodus to the nearby hills began for all who could walk or crawl, fleeing the spreading fires.

As best they could count, more than 40 percent of the hospital patients and staff had been killed. The heavy concrete construction of the building had absorbed some of the radiation, heat, and shock wave of the bomb, accounting for what survivors there were.

They scrambled up the hillside, where the once lush vegetation had been instantly seared and scorched. "Indescribable pandemonium engulfed us," Dr. Shirabe recalled.

The meeting continued. Two doctors detailed the onset of what apparently was radiation reaction ten days to a month after the bomb. Each exhibited a different reaction. Among the symptoms they described were weariness, red spots on their skin, lesions, bruises indicating hemorrhages, bloody vomiting, nasal hemorrhages, prolonged periods of elevated temperature—above 104 degrees for ten days in some cases—diarrhea, loss of tactile feeling in the legs, hair loss, and swollen gums.

"Many persons appeared disoriented for several hours, unable to recall where they were at the time of the bombing," Dr. Imafuku recalled. "I saw a student wandering aimlessly toward the main college building, which was burning furiously at the time. I had to forcibly pull back a nurse walking toward a chimney stack that seemed ready to collapse and take her up the hill. It is impossible to tell whether this was an emotional response to the terrible events they had witnessed or some brain injury. At the time we were unaware that the brain could be damaged by radiation."

Those words came back to me years later as we began to unravel in American laboratories some of the mysteries of how radiation affects the brain.

"More people died from the burns and radiation effects than from external injuries," Dr. Shirabe said. "Those who were in the open and directly exposed to the burst incurred burns over the entire body and died on the spot. An incoherent shocklike state, with marked prostration, sometimes preceded the other symptoms, which progressed to early and severe symptoms of radiation effects and death."

How well he knew, having watched his own son die.

"The deaths increased each day during the first week," Dr. Shirabe continued. "Then the number decreased in the following weeks so that by the end of a month the dying began to end."

Dr. Kimura interrupted. "There is an interesting story. In Hiroshima some children were having a diving contest and a boy who happened to be in the water when the atomic bomb fell was saved while five others who were out of the water were killed."

"That sort of thing happened here, too," Dr. Shirabe said.

The Japanese doctors sitting in that crowded classroom to give us their report disagreed with earlier American reports about the risks of exposure to radiation for those who came from outside the city to join the rescue effort.[11] The American officials had found no residual radiation level high enough to be detrimental to health. Dr. Warren's first trip to Nagasaki included an urgent need to know when it would be safe for American units to land. He sounded an all clear, and U.S. Marines came ashore September 23, 1945, six weeks after the bomb exploded.

The Japanese doctors thought the danger of residual radiation greater. They presented case studies of people who had escaped injury in the bombing only to suffer radiation sickness after entering the city on succeeding days.

I added my own contribution at this point. I had been interviewing a young woman who told me of making frequent visits to the city, beginning the day after the bombing, in search of family members. She had been in the countryside on August 9 and thereby escaped any direct exposure to radiation. On succeeding days, however, she had repeatedly crossed the hypocenter. Twelve days later, vomiting commenced, then inflammation of her gums, followed by sloughing of gum tissue, and red bleeding spots on her arms and thorax accompanied by an elevated temperature. The symptoms persisted for a month. I could explain it only as radiation sickness. Other patients told me of very different experiences. Several of them also had entered the area of the hypocenter in the days following the bombing but did not have any symptoms of radiation reaction.

I asked the doctors about burns.

There were mixed results. Some made good recoveries even though none of the new medicines such as penicillin were available. Many of the others were treated with vegetable oil in the absence of appropriate medication, and this may have been a factor in a high incidence of keloid, an elevated, thick scar tissue.

"As we did not know what treatment would be effective for the symptoms, which at first we did not know were due to radiation, many forms of treatment were used with what we had available," Dr. Shirabe said.

"While I was ill with radiation sickness, I didn't even feel like talking to friends who came to see me," Dr. Shirabe said. "However, I was greatly invigorated whenever I drank sake."

All of the doctors in the room smiled.

Before I left Nagasaki, Dr. Shirabe took me aside. "Yamazaki san," he said, "you should check out the use of alcohol for treating radiation sickness when you get back to America." It was a suggestion I have yet to investigate.

A few weeks after that meeting with the doctors and other survivors, Dr. Shirabe brought me a remarkable document. He and other medical school faculty members and fifty medical students had conducted a detailed survey of eight thousand survivors just weeks after the bombing. They completed the study in 1946. Four years later, he was handing it to me—the first medical report our team was to receive covering that critically important population. All of the other studies had been denied us under security regulations and censorship.

I later learned that this report was the basis of the Nagasaki section of the *Report of the Joint Commission on the Medical Effects of the Atomic Bomb*, still under censorship at that time.

American officials delayed the publication of detailed information about the medical consequences of the bombs until 1951, even though they had been quick to tell the world about the physical qualities of the bombs. President Truman had acted on August 11, two days after the bombing of Nagasaki, to authorize release of a report on the development of "an awesome weapon, the atomic bomb."

I was to learn most about the bombs, however, by observing what they had done to people, particularly to children.

It was August 8, 1945, the day before the bomb fell on Nagasaki. The Nagasaki University Medical School faculty, staff, and students had been called to an emergency meeting.

"This new kind of bomb may be dropped on Nagasaki, and I feel sure it won't be enough just to take refuge in air raid shelters when you hear enemy planes approaching."

The speaker was Dr. Tsuno, the dean. Quite by chance, he had seen, a day earlier, what the "new kind of bomb" had done to Hiroshima. "It is a most terrible devastation that has befallen Hiroshima," he told his colleagues. "There is not a single house or tree left undamaged in an area that encompasses three or four railway stations."

He had made his own measure of the distance. He was returning from Tokyo and a meeting of the Association of the Japan Medical Colleges, of which he was president. But when his train reached Hiroshima, it came to an unscheduled stop. The only way to continue on his journey home to Nagasaki was to walk across the city center, ravaged just the day before, to an undamaged railway station on the other side of the city.

"It's as if a huge thunderbolt struck the city and ignited a firestorm that consumed the city," he added.

On his return to Nagasaki, he quickly convened the faculty, staff, and students to share his information. Then he rushed to the mayor's office to report what he had seen.

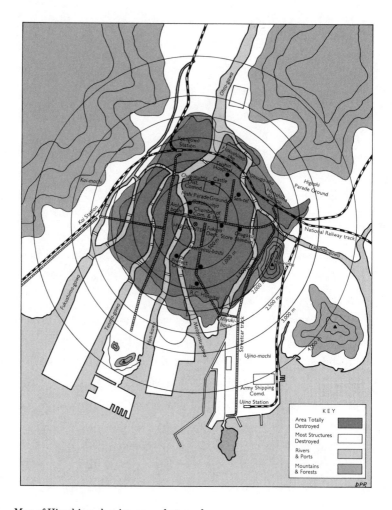

Map of Hiroshima showing areas destroyed.

Less than twenty-four hours later, the second atomic bomb was detonated. Many who heard the dean's warning were killed. The dean himself died thirteen days later.

Four years had passed when I was told this story by Dr. Tatsuichiro Akizuki, one of the heroes of the days following the bombing. He is revered, along with Dr. Shirabe, for the selfless service he rendered to the survivors.

He had not had the benefit of Dr. Tsuno's warning. When the

bomb fell, he was busy inserting a needle into the chest cavity of a patient at the tuberculosis clinic where he worked. It is a routine procedure to collapse a diseased lung. The force of the bomb threw him across the room. Despite his injuries, however, he quickly organized what seemed a tireless medical rescue service for hundreds of survivors.

How strange it is to contemplate those August events in retrospect, knowing all we now know. Aki and I had been so casual about those first news reports. Even the pilots carrying the deadly bombs to Hiroshima and Nagasaki had no way of picturing the enormous effort that had gone into building these weapons, an effort unequaled in history, or the extent of the damage the bombs would wreak. The secret of the Manhattan Project was well kept. The work must have been remarkably stressful given the constraints of secrecy and the constant concern that Nazi Germany might at any time develop its own atomic bomb.

Hiroshima was targeted with a bomb made with enriched uranium 235. It was the only uranium-based bomb. Nagasaki was hit by a bomb using plutonium 239. The incredible energy of fission was released as the plutonium was bombarded by neutrons, unleashing a chain reaction of nuclear fissions. The Nagasaki bomb weighed 4.5 tons, but it transmitted an explosive force equivalent to 22,000 tons of TNT, a force 75 percent greater than that of the Hiroshima bomb.

The energy of an atomic bomb is released in three violent ways: as thermal radiation, as nuclear radiation, and as a combination of shock wave and blast wind. "With the explosion of an atomic bomb, the maximum temperature at the burst point instantaneously reaches several million degrees centigrade," the official Japanese damage report reminds us.

One of the most vivid descriptions of these forces came from the U.S. Navy commander who targeted and observed the Nagasaki bombing aboard the plane that carried the bomb from Tinian.

The plane, a B-29 named *Bock's Car*, had taken off in the early

morning from Tinian carrying a bomb targeted for the city of Kokura. But Kokura was covered with clouds. Nagasaki was the second
choice. Seven minutes later, the plane was on target. At that very
moment, the cloud cover broke, revealing the industrial center of
the Urakami Valley. The bomb was dropped, and it detonated 503
meters (1,650 feet) above the city.

"The bomb burst with a blinding flash, and a huge column of
black smoke swirled toward us," Commander F. L. Ashworth recalled. "Out of this column of smoke there boiled a great swirling
mushroom of gray smoke, luminous with red, flashing flame, that
reached 40,000 feet in less than eight minutes.

"Below, through the clouds, we could see the pall of black smoke
ringed with fire that covered what had been the industrial area of
Nagasaki."

The thermal energy hits victims first. Traveling at the speed
of light—186,000 miles a second—this flash of light, with both
infrared and ultraviolet rays, is devastating, incinerating nearby targets and searing more distant targets. And the intense heat sets its
own array of raging fires as everything combustible in its range is
ignited.

"You can see why we have very few survivors with burns," one of
my colleagues remarked. Most of those burned within a mile of the
hypocenter died.

The immense release of nuclear radiation includes gamma rays
and neutrons, which do the most damage to living tissues. Much of
the radiation is released in the first minute. There are longer-term
energy releases as well, including fallout, which can carry radioactive particles far and wide, as we were to see most clearly later in
the Marshall Islands tests.

And then there are the shock wave and blast wind. The hurricane-
force winds make missiles of all loose objects and can tear the clothing from a body. This unprecedented destructive power, potentially

lethal for all forms of life, is catastrophic for structures near the hypocenter.

"According to the survey made by the Japanese scientists after the explosion of the atomic bombs in Hiroshima and Nagasaki, the pressure of the blast at a point directly under the epicenter (burst point) was estimated to be 4.5 to 6.7 tons per square meter in Hiroshima and 6.7 to 10 tons in Nagasaki." In those words, the report "Impact of the A-Bomb" explains why so few buildings remained standing.

We came to understand something about the three forces of the bomb—thermal, nuclear, and blast—through our clinical experiences with the survivors. Particularly instructive was our work with the seventeen women who were pregnant at the time of the bomb and were close enough to suffer radiation sickness. Only one of the seventeen had significant burns. That told us something about the force of the thermal radiation to which they had been exposed. The temperature at ground zero was at least three thousand degrees centigrade, and more than 80 percent of those within three quarters of a mile of the hypocenter died, most of them instantly or within hours.

The burn survivor in our study was Nishi, twenty-one at the time of the bomb, and in the twentieth week of her pregnancy. She was in an open field just over a mile from the hypocenter when she heard a plane. She flattened herself on the ground near a small wall.

The pain from her extensive burns was excruciating. Fortunately she was able to obtain some morphine. She lost her hair for almost a year. She had an elevated body temperature for forty days. Infections complicated the healing of her burns.

"My baby died at two months," she told us when she came for a clinical examination. From birth, the baby had been weak, had nursed poorly. Malnutrition was an overwhelming problem for everyone at the time.

There was no way then to know precisely the source of the injury, the cause of death in every case. But we came to realize that the explosive physical force of the bombs and the radiation must have been at the root of the anomalies we were seeing. And indeed, subsequent studies would make that much clearer.

The difficulty of making reliable analyses of the effects of the atomic bombs is demonstrated by some of the cases we were studying.

Fusa was six months pregnant when the bomb detonated, and her home, in Takao-machi, collapsed. She was 1,600 yards from the hypocenter. She felt violent movement of the baby within her, then no movement. Nothing. She spontaneously aborted the dead fetus the next day.

Yet Tono, age forty-four and only 1,200 yards from the hypocenter, carried her baby almost to full term but delivered an impaired child. She lived in Urakami Precinct, just east of the Mitsubishi steel and arms complex. She had already suffered the tragedy of an older son being killed in action in the war. Her six children at home were killed when the bomb exploded. She was badly bruised and lay unconscious for hours after the bomb, but suffered no burns.

Tono's baby, Toshio, was born the following February. When we examined him at the age of five, his head was extremely small. He was unable to speak, had to be fed, had no bladder control, showed evidence of heart complications, was unable to maintain the focus of his eyes, and suffered from mental retardation.

And then there was Miya, age twenty-eight, who lived in Moto-machi, within a mile of the hypocenter. Her home lay east of the Roman Catholic church and was somewhat shielded by Motomachi Hill. Miya was eight weeks pregnant. After regaining consciousness, she learned that her husband had been killed at his place of work, but her two older children, two and five years old, were apparently unharmed and her pregnancy seemed unaffected. Within a month, however, she suffered a spontaneous abortion, accompanied by such copious bleeding that a transfusion was required. And her two children began manifesting weakness and wasting. Both were dead in a matter of weeks.

Little things could save lives. A reinforced concrete wall, a small hill, a white blouse could make a difference in the effect of the bomb, shielding or deflecting the radiation. Just a few feet could spell life or death.

Kiyoko, a mother in our special study, was one of four persons seated in a room at the medical school less than eight hundred yards from the hypocenter when the bomb exploded. She was the sole survivor. All fetal movement stopped the next day, and her baby was stillborn a fortnight later. She had the full range of radiation sickness symptoms, had contusions over her entire body and burns on her right arm, but she lived. The other three who had been sitting close to her died. Why? Was it her distance from a window that saved her? Or her own vitality?

The incinerated dead and the mutilated living, the fused glass microscope slides on the medical school laboratory floor, melted metal beams, blistered ceramic tiles, instantly vaporized homes, all bore testimony of the power unleashed that August morning. Almost incalculable power.

And even now I must remind myself that this was the work of bombs that were small by comparison with the thermonuclear devices developed later.

As we began the enlarged and ambitious research program trying to detect genetic abnormalities, Mrs. Tei Murakami proved invaluable to us. She was the president of the midwives organization of Nagasaki, which included 125 practitioners. She was cheerful, open, friendly, but absolutely resolute—very much like Ma Brown, who had presided over the boardinghouse where I lived while at medical school in Milwaukee.

I first met Mrs. Murakami when I made a formal call at her home, seeking to enlist her help. The house, away from the industrial area of the city, had escaped major damage.

"Will you have some sake, Doctor?" she said almost as soon as I was seated. I demurred.

"Well, then, perhaps some of our local beer?" I could not refuse a second time.

The midwives played a decisive role in one of the most sensitive challenges of our work. We felt it would be important to conduct autopsies on any of the surviving children who might die while our study was under way, but we realized that this would be most unwelcome to grieving parents. With the quiet guidance of the midwives, the parents came to understand the potential importance of autopsies to all of them. The great majority gave their permission.

The delay in work on the clinical facilities at the Kaikan Building meant postponing the project that had been at the top of my priority list: the study of the survivors who had been exposed to the radiation while still within their mothers' wombs.

In the meantime, every effort was being made to strengthen and enlarge the genetic study that had been set in motion in Hiroshima and Nagasaki by Dr. Neel. The program included a professional examination of each newborn to look for evidence of abnormal pregnancy outcomes that might be traced to the bomb radiation exposure of their parents. This was no small task. In Nagasaki alone, five hundred to eight hundred babies were being delivered each month.

There were teams, comprised of a doctor and a nurse, to make a house call after every birth. No examining table and no laboratory were required for this work. The babies were most content being examined in the reassuring comfort of their mothers' laps. As the program expanded, it became a common sight to see the teams making their way around the city in Jeeps bearing the ABCC logo.

There was nothing any of us could do to alleviate the fear generated by our research. The routine examination of each newborn child brought home to many families for the first time the fact that the survivors were still at risk. We had no answers with which to reassure them.

There was also the risk of alienation.

"Doctor, I think we have a problem," Mrs. Murakami said to me one day.

She could be very diplomatic, and she was always polite, but she quickly came to the point. She and her fellow midwives reported that some of the medical teams appeared disdainful and less interested when their neonatal examinations took them to the modest lodgings of the poorest of the families. There was resentment among these families. I quickly relayed this concern to our doctors, many of them just out of medical school. It helped them to adopt a different approach, to be more sensitive, which in turn helped establish broader community confidence in what we were doing.

Mrs. Murakami was a respected and trusted midwife with a burgeoning practice. She had four assistants when I came to know her. All of the city's midwives were playing an essential role in that devastated city. It was they who delivered virtually all of the babies. Obstetricians were called in only if there was evidence of a major complication. And the midwives were so confident of their own expertise that they rarely felt compelled to call a doctor.

Reports of all abnormalities were brought to me for analysis. The young doctors who made the house calls were most helpful. They were eager to experience problems beyond the routine to help them prepare for their future practices, and they shared their findings with me. At the suggestion of the medical school, I set aside one afternoon each week to lecture on recent medical work and research being done in the United States. These lectures had to be delivered in Japanese, but I found I was able to meet the challenge if I met in advance with one of the Japanese doctors and reviewed the particular vocabulary required for the day's lecture.

The genetic study was under the overall direction of Dr. William J. Schull, a geneticist from Ohio State University who was based in Hiroshima. He later joined the staff of the Graduate School of Biomedical Sciences at the University of Texas, Houston, as director of the Genetics Center. I managed the program in Nagasaki alone until, months later, additional staff assistance was provided. Fortunately, Dr. Schull paid periodic visits to Nagasaki to iron out problems and to keep the work in the two cities closely coordinated.

In anticipation of expanding the program, the ABCC had been conducting a census of the entire city, with census tract maps. In this way we were able to identify and classify the survivors by their initial exposure to the bomb. This proved essential when we initiated the more detailed studies months later.

Our work in Nagasaki was made much easier by the willingness of the Japanese to integrate the research being undertaken by the ABCC with their own academic medical programs. It was a cooperative arrangement that eventually ensured the continuation of the research, under Japanese direction, to the present time.

The close cooperation between Japanese and American scientists facilitated another major research program, studying fallout to determine its impact on the population. But the fact of the matter is that I had never heard the word *fallout* before I came to Japan. I had received no information about the bomb itself, let alone the risks of fallout that had been anticipated from the time of the first test in New Mexico.

Dr. Warren had understood the potential problem. In fact, a secret evacuation plan had been developed in conjunction with the first test. The plan covered the Apache-Mescalero Indian Reservation in New Mexico and the town of Rosewell, east of Alamogordo, should that prove necessary. Fortunately, fallout from the test fell in a sparsely populated area to the northeast. But none of that information had been shared with me.

The word *fallout* was first used in my presence by a scientist from the Tracer Laboratory, sent to Nagasaki under contract with the Atomic Energy Commission.[12] I had been told to facilitate their work and to keep their visit secret. They wanted to do research in the Nishiyama Valley and came with instruments to detect radiation and gear to collect samples for more extensive laboratory studies in the United States.

I quickly learned what they wanted to do. Earlier investigations had concluded that the fallout from the Nagasaki bomb fell mostly in the Nishiyama Valley. Mount Kompira, which towers over Nagasaki, had shielded the upper Nishiyama Valley from the direct effect of the bomb's radiation. If there were contamination in that area, it would have come solely from the "black rain," the bomb's fallout, not directly from the bomb. This provided an opportunity for a thorough study of fallout.

The visiting scientists explained to me that the bomb's plutonium had fragmented into highly radioactive particles at the instant of the explosion. These were swept upward by the incredible heat, part of the mushroom cloud that was described by those aboard the American bomber. With condensation of the superheated air, some of these elements were incorporated with the smoke and dust into rain droplets and fell back to earth—the black rain of the bomb.

This was also an opportunity for me to see something of rural Japan. Even though the affected area lay close to the city, life was completely different there. I would visit with the farmers over a cup of tea in the open-hearth kitchens of their simple dwellings, marveling at the fertility of their farmland, which was apparently untouched by the atomic bomb. Only four years after the black rain had fallen, the land was lush with eggplants, sweet potatoes, and other crops.

The farmers were cooperative. Guided by sensitive counters, we began collecting samples from rain spouts, straw roofing, and mud deposits. The research team received permission to drain a reservoir to study the accumulated silt. All these materials were bound for laboratory analysis in the United States.

I never saw the results of their work, although I learned their conclusions indirectly from published reports. Contrary to expectations, the research found no long-term deleterious effects from the fallout. There was a transient elevation of white blood cells in children. Subsequent studies by the Nagasaki University Medical School as well as the Radiation Effects Research Foundation also indicated that the relatively small total radiation exposure from the fallout apparently was insufficient to cause death or long-term injury. But research continues to this day. And so does the controversy.[13]

The scientific findings contradict some anecdotal material included in books and poems written in the post-bomb period in Japan. Many who suffered the devastation of the bombs remain convinced that residual radiation, both in the area of the hypocenter and in more distant areas affected only by fallout, had serious biological consequences for the survivors.

There is little argument, however, about the difference between the relatively benign fallout of Hiroshima and Nagasaki, and the highly toxic fallout generated by the Marshall Islands test.

We did not have to wait for the remodeling of the Kaikan Building to study the impact of the bomb on the human eye. In yet another gesture of generosity and cooperation, the Nagasaki University Medical School turned over to us the first of its clinics to be reconstructed after the war.

The availability of this clinic coincided with increasing concern among scientists about the impact of radiation on eyesight, inspired in part by the recent discovery of high cataract incidence among cyclotron workers who had been regularly exposed to forms of radiant energy similar to those emitted by the bomb—including neutrons and gamma rays. We needed to look for evidence of lesions of the cornea, iris, lens, and retina that could impair vision.

The research, centered in Hiroshima, was led by three distinguished ophthalmologists: Dr. David Cogan, of the Harvard University School of Medicine; Dr. Sam Kimura from the University of California, San Francisco; and Dr. Hiroshi Ikui, of the Kyushu University School of Medicine.[14] Teamwork between Japanese and American physicians was our standard practice.

Their work, implemented by the medical school faculty, found that cataracts were the first of the delayed effects to develop in the body as a whole. Some cases of discrete lens lesions were found. But we were surprised to determine that the number of survivors with impaired vision was relatively small.[15]

War came back to East Asia on June 25, 1950, six months after our arrival in Nagasaki. North Korea had invaded South Korea, and the military force of the United States, with allied nations, was being deployed under the banner of the United Nations to resist the aggression.

The impact of the Korean War on Nagasaki was enormous. Nagasaki is only 150 miles from Korea, and just 40 miles from Sasebo, which came to serve as a major staging area and debarkation port for American troops. My help was requested by the U.S. Army physician in the area as he tried to piece together health care for the children of American servicemen quartered nearby. The nearest U.S. military hospital was 100 miles away. I found myself making night calls on sick American children who were a very long way from home.

My bitterest memories of the Battle of the Bulge, the slaughter in the Ardennes, came back to me in succeeding weeks as the death and casualty toll of the American servicemen mounted. These men had just arrived in Japan, settling in for what they thought would be a routine assignment, when the Korean War started. And they were the first American military personnel to go into action. None returned to the Nagasaki area while we remained in Japan. Many died or were captured. One of the divisions to which they were assigned lost seven thousand of its ten thousand men — dead or captured — in a five-day battle. Their families had to pack up for desperately lonely returns to the United States.

My most direct contact with that war came in the form of a three-day meeting with the admiral commanding the American amphibious forces. I had been instructed to arrange a thorough briefing for him on the bombing of Nagasaki. The admiral came to Nagasaki aboard his command ship, with escorting navy combat vessels. My colleagues and I presented a full picture of what the atomic bomb had done. There was still evidence of the physical damage for them to see; we provided graphic examples of the human cost.

I can only guess at the reasons why that briefing was requested. Whatever the reasons, I took great satisfaction in having had that opportunity to present in detail to senior military decision makers the real consequences, the true cost of using this sort of weapon.

I did treat one casualty of the Korean War. One day I was asked to board the British freighter *Glenarm* to help a crew member injured when the ship had been strafed by North Korean fighter planes.[16]

At this time, in the early summer of 1950, the work of the ABCC was about to take a positive leap forward. Drs. Stan and Phyllis Wright, pediatricians from the University of Rochester, arrived in September at the Nagasaki Railroad Station, their enthusiasm evidently undiminished by the typhoon that was raging as they stepped from the train. They moved in next door to us, a splendid addition both to the work of the commission and to our personal lives.

They arrived just before the remodeling of the Kaikan Building was completed. As we sat down together to plan the next step, I realized once again that those nine months of delays had not been time wasted. What I had learned in that period had enriched my understanding of the people of Nagasaki and would serve us well as we targeted the research program.

Still at the forefront of my thoughts was the study of radiation's adverse influence on fetal development, the very work that I had plotted out with Dr. Warkany at the Children's Hospital Research Foundation at the University of Cincinnati before I left for Japan. Two other programs were already moving ahead. The genetic study under Dr. Schull was being expanded to provide for follow-up examinations of 20 percent of the newborns to determine if there were any changes or new findings at the ages of eight to ten months. And we were scheduling, as soon as the new clinic was ready, follow-up examinations of all the children in whom we had identified abnormalities.

With the Wrights on staff, we were able to expand the lectures I had been giving on American medicine. The talks were extended to include evening discussions of research being reported in current American medical journals. The young Japanese doctors in attendance responded with an exchange of songs and stories at the end of the sessions, cementing the close and cooperative relationship that had been developing among us.

Genji Matsuda, one of those young doctors with a strong singing voice, was to bring international recognition to our staff. He won a two-year fellowship at the California Institute of Technology in Pasadena, working under Nobel Prize winner Linus Pauling, and then went on to do advanced research at the Max Planck Institute in Munich. He returned to Nagasaki to become chairman of biochemistry and then dean of the medical school before his retirement. We knew Matsuda was going to be a success when he made a complex cardiac diagnosis on one of his first house calls in the genetic survey.

At this point, the ABCC staff comprised 250 persons, almost all of them Japanese. I was happy to have the Wrights to share the administrative responsibilities of this expanding operation and their professional help in discerning the long-term medical consequences for the survivors. But I knew the sense of isolation that was part of the Nagasaki operation for Americans, especially when compared with life in Hiroshima, with its large staff of American medical personnel.

I did not want them to leave. So Aki and I did our best to show off the attractions of Nagasaki and the area around it that we had come to appreciate. We introduced the Wrights to the special joys of the country inns and Japanese cuisine. They took to sleeping between quilted futons with grace, and mastered the *hashi*—chopsticks— while learning to sit cross-legged on the tatami floor mats.

Encouraged by the smooth-running staff and expanded medical crew, I resubmitted my proposal to study children who had been in the womb when the bomb exploded. The ABCC Research Committee approved the plan and instructed that it be extended to include Hiroshima.

Our earlier ABCC census provided us with most of the information we needed to locate survivors. Japanese officials readily agreed to provide the missing data by including in the national census questions that would locate survivors who had moved away from Hiroshima and Nagasaki. Thus we had identified those we needed to contact to do the research. We were ready to go.

My own time in Nagasaki was running out, and I realized, as I worked out the final parameters of the study, that none of us would know all the answers for years to come.

We decided to use two groups of children for the intrauterine study. The most important group would be those who were in the womb and within two thousand meters of the hypocenter at the moment of detonation, and whose mothers had developed the triad of radiation disease symptoms: loss of hair, bleeding skin lesions, and throat and gum ulcerations. The other would be children who were in the womb at the moment of detonation but were four to five thousand meters from the hypocenter — a control group, as it were.

We were also continuing our studies of children caught in proximity to the blast. In the end, we were able to identify only 134 surviving children who had been within a thousand-meter radius, and only 12 who had been within five hundred meters.

We needed to keep careful track of the development of the 134 survivors for comparison with those exposed while fetuses. At that time we had not yet confirmed that the risk of radiation damage is even greater for the fetus than for children after birth. Nor had we devised research techniques that would allow us to differentiate between defects caused by radiation of the fetus and defects caused by the trauma of the bomb or such other factors as infection and the malnutrition prevalent in Japan during and immediately after the war.

As we planned our research, I recalled a conversation with Dr. Warren on the eve of my departure. He had emphasized the importance of watching for symptoms that might develop long afterward. Instant whole body radiation, such as that caused by the bomb, was new in the annals of medicine. Some consequences might not be known until we had completed careful observations of the survivors over their entire lifetimes.

I needed to know more about the impact of the bomb on the children. The description from the doctors' panel at University Hospital said much about the trauma that everyone had suffered in terms of separation, loss, radiation, and death. But, as a pediatrician, I knew that much more had to be understood if we were to capture the full impact on young people.

Dr. Shirabe responded to my concern with a quick reference. "I know just the person for you to talk to," he said. He was right. It was to be one of the most compelling interviews I had in all my time in Nagasaki.

I was directed to a tiny shack, constructed of scrap metal and old pieces of wood, on a hillside. There, on a simple bed, lay Dr. Takashi Nagai. His makeshift shelter was like many that still covered areas of Nagasaki four years after the bomb. In the aftermath of that attack, there had been eighty thousand homeless.

Dr. Nagai could not come to any meetings at the hospital. He was suffering from leukemia, possibly brought on by radiation exposure before the bomb while working as an assistant professor of radiology, but almost certainly complicated by massive radiation exposure on August 9. He was with Dr. Shirabe at the hospital when the bomb detonated, and he had been seriously cut by flying glass. Dr. Shirabe had sutured the stubbornly bleeding blood vessel behind Dr. Nagai's ear as they fled to the hills hours after the bombing.

Dr. Nagai's two children were with their grandparents in the countryside when the bomb fell, and survived. His wife was killed, and their home demolished, so he had made this shack to shelter himself and the two surviving children.

From this simple place he ministered to the wounded. And, pen in hand, he had become a voice of the victims. His book, *The Bells of Nagasaki*, held up by American occupation censors for three years, was published in Japanese in 1949, in English in 1984. A second book, in which he edited the recollections of the children, was to become my primer as we prepared to study the pediatric implications of the bomb. *Living Beneath the Atomic Cloud Testimonies* was not made available in English translation until it was published by Wilmington College in Ohio in 1983.

As I sat beside him in the shack, he told me how he had come to seek those recollections of the children:

"So much of the story told by the survivors is so incredible that the reality of a nuclear explosion might be more believable if told through the voices of the children themselves, telling us what they saw through their guileless eyes, and how they simply felt as the world they knew suddenly was shattered."

He asked the children at the nearby Yamazato Elementary School, the few who had survived, to tell their stories. They were his neighbors, classmates of his children. The little ones told their stories to teachers. The older ones wrote down their stories.

Fujio Tsujimoto was five and enjoying the playground when he heard a distant airplane.

"I grabbed my grandmother by the hand and ran toward the shelter. 'Enemy plane!' yelled the watchman on the roof of the school building as he struck the bell. 'Look out!' People on the playground came running straight for the shelter. I was the first to plunge into the deepest part of the shelter. But at that moment, flash, I was blown against the wall by the force of the explosion.

"After a while," he continued, "I peered from out of the shelter. I found people scattered all over the playground. The ground was covered almost entirely with bodies. Most of them looked dead and lay still. Here and there, however, some were thrashing their legs or raising their arms. Those who were able to move came crawling into the shelter. Soon the shelter was crowded with the wounded. Around the school all the town was on fire. My house also was burning fiercely.

"My brother and sisters were late in coming into the shelter; so they were burnt and crying. . . . Half an hour later my mother appeared at last. She was covered with blood. . . . I will never forget how happy I was as I clung to my mother. We waited and waited for Father, but he never appeared. . . . Even those who had survived died in agony one after another. My younger sister died the next day. My mother, she also died the next day. And then my older brother. I thought I would die, too, because the people around me lying beside each other in the shelter were dying one by one. Yet, because my grandmother and I had been in the deepest part of the shelter, we apparently had not been exposed to the radiation and in the end we were saved."

I read on.

About a dying mother who somehow summoned superhuman strength to lift a beam that a group of men could not budge, and by so doing freed her baby daughter even as the fires burned closer.

About the bewilderment of children who had been sent to the safety of the countryside, and, coming home after the bomb, found nothing.

"We got the news that the A-bomb had been dropped on Nagasaki and Father had been killed at his company," Junko Miyata, four years old when the bomb fell, told Dr. Nagai. "So we came back to Nagasaki. Our house was ruined. My doll was broken."

Kayano Nagai, the professor's daughter, was five when the bomb detonated, safe at Koba with her grandparents. Her account was this:

"My house had been large and Mother used to be there, but now I found everything in ashes and nothing remaining. We built a house of tin in the ruins. We put two window panes to make the room brighter. We slept there, but it was so cramped that I was troubled by my brother kicking me. Though our house was completed, Mama didn't come back to us. Now Father is sick in bed all day. He can move his hands but the rest of his body he is unable to move. When he goes out, he must be carried on a stretcher. I hope Father can walk soon. Then I'd like to go to the mountains hand in hand with my father to draw pictures."

And I began to hear stories myself.

Hitoshi told me that he and his friend Kishikawa, student workers at the Mitsubishi ordnance plant, had fallen asleep in the shelter. They had gone there during the morning air raid warning and did not hear the all clear. They were awakened by the frenzied voices of people outside.

"When we walked out of the shelter, we were stunned by what we saw. Where there had been homes, flowers, and trees surrounding the factory, nothing remained except the rubble, the fire, and the smoldering embers. The dead, burned, and injured were everywhere."

Hitoshi's sister escaped death because, a second before the bomb, she had crawled into the bomb shelter under their house searching for a piece of candy. The house, some 330 yards from the hypocenter, was reduced to ashes. Over those ashes, Hitoshi, his brother, and his sister built a shack for themselves, shelter for three orphans of the bomb.

Toshiko Murakami — not her real name — had been assembling a torpedo guidance mechanism at the Mitsubishi plant when the bomb detonated. She was sixteen. "Suddenly the room was illuminated by a bright orange-yellow hue followed by a roaring sound and then a blast of powerful wind," she told me.[17]

"I felt an agonizing pain on the side of the face and neck facing the window, and glass splinters pierced me. My face was burned, as was the exposed part of my head, neck, and arms," she added, showing the black pigmentation that remained four years later. Her white shirt apparently protected her abdomen.

She and a friend rescued another worker and carried her to safety in the worker's undamaged home nearby. The river was filled with charred bodies as Toshiko made her way to her own home, only to find it destroyed.

As the fire intensified, the two women feared again for their lives. Toshiko found herself so weak she could scarcely walk. Finally, her companion said: "It's no use for both of us to die. Save yourself." And she ran on, leaving Toshiko by the road.

"Later, people have asked me whether I was bitter toward my classmate at being abandoned. I replied — not at all. That was a time when survival, self-preservation, were so overpowering that no one can deny life to another person."

She turned to me then and added: "You know about that, Doctor. You were once a soldier on the battlefield. You know what I mean."

An acquaintance later guided Toshiko to where her sister lay dying in the basement of a school building.

"I found my older sister hardly recognizable among the dying and the dead," Toshiko continued. "Her face was swollen and burnt, her body pierced by glass and wood splinters which I pulled out. I had developed a mucousy diarrhea from the first day and was very uncomfortable and tore bits of my clothing to care for my toilet. But I stayed with my sister. The situation in the basement was appalling: the desperate condition of the victims, the overpowering stench of diarrhea, the vomitus, the excrement, and the putrefying wounds, and burns. Wriggling maggots appeared in my burns."

When help finally came, the rescuers refused to evacuate Toshiko. They feared her diarrhea was a symptom of sekiri, a highly contagious and sometimes fatal disease common in the area, and they did not want to risk infecting the others. Several days passed before

Nagasaki the day after, August 10, 1945, at the main intersection of Matsuyama township a quarter mile north of the hypocenter. Hitoshi's home was in Oka-machi, the township just to the east of Matsuyama. To escape the encroaching fire on the day of the bombing, Hitoshi climbed the western slope of the valley in search of his family. As he descended the valley, crossing the Urakami River to Matsuyama on the way to his home, he came upon the massive devastation and panicked at the thought of what might have happened to his family. Photo by Yosuke Yamahata.

she was found by family members and evacuated to a nearby island where a medical facility was still operating.

Years later, I learned another chapter in her sad story. Her engagement was broken by the family of her fiancé because they feared the stigma of bringing into the family a *hibakusha*, an atomic bomb survivor. I would learn more about the discrimination against survivors when I returned to Japan in 1989. Fortunately for the survivors, the Japanese government had by then established effective social services for them.

This anecdotal material served me in two ways. Perhaps most importantly, I was inspired to move quickly to get the research program operational in Nagasaki. As a pediatrician, it was reassuring to move beyond statistics and be dealing with real people, people who needed all the help and understanding we could provide. The case histories also served to underscore the importance of keeping our work open to change, for there was no way to predict where our findings would lead us.

I had a personal commitment to the research on the children who were in their mothers' wombs when the bomb detonated. I did not know then how helpful that research would prove in understanding the forces of the bombs themselves. But it was already clear that we needed to look carefully at all the survivors, including those children who had been caught in the radiation, for we knew very, very little at that time about the effects of radiation on adults and children, let alone the unborn.

As spring flowered in our garden, it became clear that I had to cut short my work. I asked for permission to leave three months early because Aki was affected by a disabling illness during the rainy summer months and the typhoon season. None of our medical staff and none of our visiting physicians were able to diagnose the cause. It was a most unpleasant experience for Aki. But she maintained her sense of humor: because of her sensitivity to humidity and rainfall, she was able to forecast rain for staff members contemplating picnics. We decided to sail back to the United States on the ship on which we came, the *President Cleveland*.

Two uncertainties haunted me as I left Japan. First, the future of the ABCC's work in Nagasaki was in doubt. One AEC committee, after only a cursory examination in January, had recommended its termination.[18] Another AEC committee was completing a thorough examination of the program even as we were packing.[19] And there was also a sobering uncertainty for me personally. I had no job to which I could return. I was fascinated by the research I had begun, but I was also eager to start treating children in a normal pediatric practice.

Above all, I was committed to the challenge to extend our knowledge of the long-term effects of radiation—a challenge accepted with the fervent hope that the world would never again have to deal with the results of nuclear attack.

The two-week voyage home aboard the *President Cleveland* was a blessing indeed. Paul was now an active two-year-old toddler, and Aki and I were kept on the move. But we had time to enjoy the luxury of the ship. And I had not a single symptom of the seasickness that had troubled me when I was making my first career decision fifteen years before.

I had become increasingly tense during the final months in Nagasaki. I was inundated with visiting committees, administrative problems, staff adjustments, and a growing concern that all of this work might soon be abandoned as the American government faced the cost of the Korean War. I had developed abdominal pains as the stress mounted. But the two weeks at sea proved to be marvelous therapy.

Our first days back in the United States were spent in California with Dr. Kimura, who had done the cataract research in Nagasaki. He had returned to his work in ophthalmology at the University of California at San Francisco. His hospitality was the first of many warm welcomes I would receive from the network of physicians we had come to know while working with the bomb survivors and their children.

Vacation time was over the instant our train reached Los Angeles and we made our way to my parents' home in the rectory at St. Mary's Church. A plane ticket to Washington awaited. A week of meetings at the Atomic Energy Commission had already been scheduled for me. For the first time in my life, I took on the role of lobbyist, of advocate.

My primary concern in doing so was to counter the termination of the entire program in Nagasaki recommended by the AEC committee that had visited us briefly in January. And then I had to find support for the program, trusting that the second and more thorough AEC survey done in June would have established the importance of what we were doing. In the balance were all the elements of the program, including the genetic follow-up examinations and the screening of those exposed as fetuses.

Dr. John Bugher, then deputy director of the AEC's Division of Biology and Medicine, asked me to present the perspective of the work of the ABCC in Nagasaki as seen from my position as physician in charge.[20] I held nothing back. In my presentation, I outlined the extraordinary findings that were just beginning to come from our painstaking work. I reminded the AEC members of the remarkable staff of Japanese doctors who had become part of the ongoing research program.

Ultimately, the decision was made to continue the work, all of it, on a permanent basis. And so it is that the work continues today, a recognition that many answers may not come even in the lifetimes of the bomb survivors. I was gratified, although I suspect my own influence may have been limited. I later learned that the strongest advocate for continued research had been General Douglas MacArthur, who had been relieved three months earlier as supreme commander of the Allied powers. His recognition of the importance of our work was indeed welcome.

Had the research been terminated then, as the first AEC committee had recommended, there would have been serious repercussions. For the Japanese, it would have been painful beyond words, indicating our disregard for the consequences of these lethal American weapons. And for the rest of the world, so troubled and uncertain about the effects of this new weapon, it would have been seen as an unforgivable lost opportunity.

Three interesting jobs were offered to me in the succeeding weeks. Dr. Wilbur Davison, chairman of pediatrics at the Duke University Medical School, asked me to join his faculty. He had been on the AEC team that visited Nagasaki in June, just as I was leaving. I was offered a job as staff pediatrician at the hospital of the Los Alamos National Research Laboratory in New Mexico. And Dr. Warren offered me a post on the faculty of the UCLA Medical School, then just being organized.

I chose UCLA and was appointed an instructor in pediatrics, the third physician to be hired in the department.

From the beginning Dr. Warren encouraged my interest in radiation exposure. His work on radiation safety throughout the development of the atomic bomb, and his survey in Japan immediately after the bombing of Hiroshima and Nagasaki, qualified him as one of the world's experts.

Aki and I were delighted to find a conveniently located apartment to rent. We ordered some basic furniture and were ready to move in when the landlord had second thoughts about introducing a Japanese-American family to his neighborhood. When we went to sign the lease, he told us the agreement had been canceled.

Aki and I decided to visit the prospective neighbors. "Who doesn't want me as a neighbor?" I asked each person. "Not me," each one responded. "We'd love to have a professional man living among us," one replied. But we were not convinced, and I just could not subject Aki and Paul to an uncertain welcome.

The university quickly put me in touch with a faculty member who was moving from his home in nearby Van Nuys. He readily offered us a lease with an option to buy. We moved in to the warmest of welcomes from the neighbors. All of the fathers in the neighborhood were, like me, veterans of the war. We have been there ever since.

We came to this home a family of three. It was not long, though, before our two daughters, Kathy and Carol, were born and we were a family of five.

The UCLA Medical School was under construction at that time, which meant that there were no laboratories in which to launch the work I was so eager to do. The staff was still being recruited and organized. Even so, as soon as I outlined my hope to study fetal brain damage resulting from the Nagasaki bomb, I was promised total support and cooperation. Members of every specialty encouraged me to undertake the work and promised their own cooperation. Today, with different financial pressures and demands on researchers, the informal and cooperative research effort that was constructed at UCLA could hardly be duplicated.

My initial work with animals was centered at the Long Beach Naval Hospital because there were no facilities for it at UCLA. My tutor through that period was Dr. Horace Magoun, who took time to help me work out the necessary animal research even though he was then deeply involved with the task of organizing UCLA's Brain Research Institute.

I quickly realized that I had a lot to learn, not just about brain research but about working with experimental animals as well. Some monkeys were made available to me at the Long Beach facility, but not for long. One monkey escaped from the X-ray table, leading to a massive hunt through hospital corridors, and another died of an unexpected drug reaction. The staff suggested I work with guinea pigs. In succeeding years, rats proved the most useful for our work. All of that work led me to appreciate the crucial importance of experimental animals in protecting the health of babies and children, who, even then, were being needlessly exposed to hazardous levels of radiation.

Doubts developed in my mind about being a full-time researcher, however, and these doubts coincided with appeals from the Japanese-

American community doctors in Los Angeles to open a pediatric practice.

Eighteen months after accepting a faculty position at UCLA, I was allowed to change to part-time clinical status at the university. I was free to open a general pediatric practice while teaching and doing research one day a week. At the age of thirty-six, I was finally doing what I had dreamed of doing for so long: working as a pediatrician.

I must have been one of the most-traveled physicians in sprawling Los Angeles. At one time I had two pediatric offices, one in Little Tokyo, in the central downtown area, and another not far from St. Mary's. Even when I narrowed the practice to a single office, I made calls at several hospitals spread from East Los Angeles to Santa Monica and I had to be under way by six o'clock in the morning.

Echoes of Nagasaki: One of my first patients was a little boy whose abnormally small head became evident as I completed my first examination. But this was not the result of nuclear radiation. It was a rare anomaly in which the skull fuses prematurely, reducing the potential for brain growth. For this boy, unlike the victims of radiation, there was a surgical remedy and the assurance of a normal life.

I did not know at the time that one of the young mothers who brought her children to me in Los Angeles was herself a survivor of the Nagasaki bomb. She was an American of Japanese ancestry who had been trapped there on a visit when the war began, her life made miserable by suspicions that she and her family were American spies. I suppose the bitterness of that experience explains why she did not share the story with me when she first came to my office. She later spoke freely of her feelings and her decision never to return to Nagasaki.

The structure of the factory where she had worked in Nagasaki shielded her from the full impact of the bomb. She recalled suffering only diarrhea, not other forms of radiation illness. She had been a little more than a mile from the hypocenter. Most of the serious radiation effects occurred inside that range.

Forty-nine years after the exposure, she shows no evidence of life-threatening injury. And her two children, born more than a decade later, show no evidence of genetic damage. But they know, as I do, that there is no certainty that abnormalities will not emerge later in the span of their lifetimes, or in the generations to come.

My shift from full-time to part-time researcher did not change my close relationship with the UCLA faculty. Much of the early brain radiation research had to be done at night. The UCLA Medical School was up and running by then, but the only radiation equipment available to us was the same equipment used for treatment and diagnosis of the patients at the medical center. It was available for my research only after the last patient had been treated. That meant arriving at the medical center after ten o'clock in the evening, often working till midnight, and making absolutely sure that none of the rats escaped to upset the human patients. Only when the Laboratory of Nuclear Medicine and Radiation Biology opened five years later was I able to work on a more flexible schedule.

The work received decisive assistance from many on the UCLA staff. I like to list them to demonstrate the extraordinary diversity of specialties they brought to the work. Dr. John Adams, busy organizing the pediatrics department, guided me in starting the animal research. Dr. Leslie R. Bennett, head of the nuclear medicine program, designed the overall research. And we had the special enthusiasm of Dr. Carmine D. Clemente, already working on radiation effects on the brain.

"Let's give it a whirl," Dr. Clemente would say emphatically when he returned from England two years later and joined our work.

Dr. Ole A. Schjeide, an embryologist with a background in biochemistry, analyzed the biochemical alterations accompanying the changes we observed. Dr. Jean de Vellis looked at cellular enzyme injury. We had the benefit of the work of Dr. Marta Billings, a radiologist, and Dr. G. Baldwin Lamson, a pathologist, observing long-term effects of radiation administered in early life.

When head irradiation resulted in motor function impairment, Dr. Earl Eldred and an associate undertook a special study to determine if lesions could be localized in muscles as well as in brain tissue. Dr. Benedict Cassen, a physicist, designed a special cone to beam the X rays narrowly on the fetal brain tissue of the rats. Dr. George Mason, an obstetrician, joined us on his day off to perform delicate intraabdominal surgery to expose the heads of the rat fetuses so that we could target the radiation on brain tissue, an essential element of our search for an understanding of how the atomic bomb affected the developing human brain.

This impressive teamwork continued for fifteen years, even longer for some of us. Dr. David Mosier, a pediatric endocrinologist, was still at work thirty years later investigating the neuroendocrine aspects of brain injury related to growth impairment.

All of this was a sobering lesson for me, trained as a pediatrician, and not as a researcher. When I set out to do research, I had no idea of the complexity of the project and of the need to mobilize persons from so many specialties. I came to understand that successful research is indeed a collaborative effort, not a solo experience. I also came to value basic research as an equal partner with the physician ministering to the sick at a hospital bedside.

My investigation of brain damage was enhanced in those years by clinical work with brain-damaged children. I began by attending the weekly neurology clinic with Dr. Margaret Jones at UCLA. Later, I assisted for years at the neurology clinic led by Dr. Robert Sedgewick at Children's Hospital in Los Angeles. Pediatric neurology was only beginning then to take hold as a subspecialty.

Early in our work we identified specific reactions related to two things: the age of the animal irradiated, and the dosage of the radiation. The immature, developing brain is far more vulnerable to radiation damage than a more mature brain, thus the particular vulnerability of the brain in the fetus.

My role on the team was to analyze the behavior of the laboratory rats. For each rat I charted unusual gait and motor function, ability to right itself, tremors, abnormal head size, irregular behavior, and seizures. I kept thinking back to that day in Nagasaki when, for the first time, I had observed a child with similar neurological manifestations after exposure to radiation.

Singularly impressive in our work was the evidence of the vulnerability of the developing brain. Brain lesions revealed how radiation dismantles the orderly and precise arrangements of layers of brain cells, scrambling them into a tangled confusion of cells of altered size while decimating other brain cells. We made some of the earliest findings of biochemical injury resulting from irradiation of the developing brain.

Our research was moving ahead at an exciting pace at the very moment, in July 1957, when my eye fell on a few lines in the newsletter of the American Academy of Pediatricians. An ad hoc committee on the effects of radiation on children was being formed. I quickly offered my services. Three months later, I was beginning what would be thirteen years of work on the committee as the academy played an increasingly influential role in informing physicians about the perils of radiation to children.[21]

To this day, the American Academy of Pediatricians provides vigorous leadership on behalf of the health of children, working to protect them not just from infection and disease, but also from abuse and a whole range of environmental hazards. The academy's commitment to high-quality care for children and political action on behalf of children, sponsoring reform legislation and educating the public, sets a standard for all professional organizations, in my view.

At the outset, the new committee acknowledged that information regarding radiation was developing at such a rapid pace that few if any practicing pediatricians could keep up. We had to develop ways to keep them better informed.

The effectiveness of the committee in its early years was in large measure due to the leadership of such men as Dr. Robert Aldrich, first director of the National Institute of Child Health and Development; Dr. Lee Farr, chairman of the Committee on Atomic Casualties; Dr. Paul Wehrle, later president of the academy, and Dr. Robert W. Miller, chief of epidemiology at the National Cancer Institute, who had served in Hiroshima with ABCC.

Because of general ignorance of the hazards, X rays were being used widely with virtually no regulation.[22] Children were being needlessly exposed to radiation—even shoe stores used X-ray machines as devices for fitting shoes. Most doctors, relying on the effectiveness of X rays for diagnosis and the management of diseases, were not aware of the importance of limiting exposure.

"Radiological exposure during fetal or neonatal periods of life leaves a maximum time span for the development of [consequential abnormalities]," Dr. Farr had told us, an urgent reminder of the lifelong dangers facing a child exposed in its earliest months.

As a first step, we set out standards to limit the amounts of radiation used, to shield the X rays and isotopes to reduce the area of exposure, and to outline procedures whereby radiation equipment could be regularly monitored and adjusted under the supervision of certified technicians.

Dr. Fred Silverman, the pediatric radiologist with whom I had worked at Children's Hospital in Cincinnati, played an influential role in winning support from other radiologists. I had known him first for his pioneering work using X rays to detect evidence of child abuse.

Our interest turned almost immediately to broader risks. Dr. Farr made sure that Nagasaki and Hiroshima were on the agenda, and he also helped us focus on the fallout risks from the Marshall Islands tests. As medical director of the Brookhaven National Laboratory, he had dispatched research teams to the islands after the ill-fated test on March 1, 1954, just three years before our committee was formed.

That first hydrogen bomb created a force almost seven hundred times greater than that of the Nagasaki atomic bomb. And it created for the first time extensive, deadly fallout that irradiated some of the islanders in its path.

When I left Nagasaki I had thought I would never have to deal with another population injured by nuclear weapons. But now, nine years after atomic bombs were dropped on Japan, yet another population had been made the victims of an even more menacing and more powerful weapon.

My particular responsibility on the academy's radiation committee was to maintain current records on the status of the research on Hiroshima, Nagasaki, and the Marshall Islands. Those facts and figures told us one thing: We must not delay in sounding a global alarm about the hazards of radiation in all its forms, and the particular vulnerability of children.

What a paradox that our hopes for setting safer peacetime standards regarding radiation emerged to a considerable extent from research based on the effects of the deadliest weaponry known to humanity.

But even as we tried to focus attention on the hazards of radiation, the Great Powers were continuing to generate environmental radiation with their atmospheric nuclear testing. The first timid steps toward an atmospheric test ban did not come until 1963.

Almost forty years passed between my first and last visits to Japan. By any measure, those four decades produced remarkable advances in our knowledge of the effects of radiation on children and the consequences of radiation for life on earth. I was fortunate to find myself at the very center of some of the work.

The answers we found responded to grave questions about the short-term effects of radiation, including the toll of fallout. The answers that continued to elude us had to do with the long-term genetic consequences. And we are still accumulating data on the delayed effects represented by some cancers appearing only as the survivors reach old age.

I was in an enviable position to hear what was going on through my position with the American Academy of Pediatrics and through my ongoing research at UCLA. Earlier studies, withheld under military censorship for no good reason, were also becoming available. And the tragedy of the Marshall Islands test disaster gave us for the first time an understanding of how fallout can affect humans.

In 1953, at an AEC symposium for embryologists, I was able to present the first findings of the work we had done in Nagasaki. We met at Oak Ridge, Tennessee, in a structure overlooking the giant laboratory complex where weapons-grade uranium and the techniques for the production of plutonium had been developed. I had come to one of the birthplaces of the Hiroshima and Nagasaki bombs. Unknown to the country and the world, a city of seventy thousand arose there during World War II, hidden in the rolling hills and valleys of Tennessee, a crucial part of the strenuous effort to meet the German challenge.

The report we presented at Oak Ridge covered the thirty pregnant women who had suffered extensive radiation illness after exposure to the Nagasaki bomb. They had been within 2,200 yards of the hypocenter and had somehow survived.

In this group, 43 percent of the pregnancies ended in death through spontaneous abortion, stillbirth, or neonatal or infant death; 17 percent of the babies were born with abnormalities, including mental retardation, eye defects, and urinary incontinence. Forty percent were born with no significant observable abnormalities. Among the survivors, the mean head circumference, body height, and weight were significantly reduced.

We had to acknowledge that we could not specify the degree to which radiation had been responsible for the morbidity and mortality. These women had suffered extensive trauma, burns, malnutrition, and infection, each of which could have had a role in the negative pregnancy outcomes.

The UCLA study was designed to find specifically the effect of radiation on the developing human brain. In the laboratory, we were able to separate the deleterious impact of radiation from other factors such as trauma, burns, and malnutrition. Our brain damage study group at UCLA had received international recognition in 1958, when we were at the halfway point in our work, and a paper on our findings was part of the proceedings of the Second United Nations Conference on the Peaceful Uses of Atomic Energy in Geneva.

The brain research we had commenced at UCLA in 1952 demonstrated with precision the relative vulnerability of the developing fetal brain as contrasted with the greater resistance to damage of the adult brain. Major contributions had come from Dr. George Plummer, a University of Rochester pediatrician, and Dr. Robert W.

Miller, with whom I had worked at the American Academy of Pediatrics. It was Dr. Plummer, working in Hiroshima, who discovered the reduced head size and mental retardation among children exposed in utero within a radius of about three quarters of a mile of the hypocenter.

Dr. Miller, following up this work at Hiroshima, had been able to determine that the maximum vulnerability to radiation damage occurs from the eighth through the fifteenth week after conception. This is a period of intense development of the brain with the greatest proliferation of neurons and their migration to the cerebral cortex. There is reduced vulnerability in the eight weeks after this critical period; and fetuses in the first eight weeks after conception are least vulnerable.

We had a case study to demonstrate that vulnerability.

Tetsuro was born seven months after the bombing. His mother had been scarcely half a mile from the hypocenter. He had been conceived fourteen weeks before the bombing. That placed him, when the bomb fell, in the gestation period when the brain is most vulnerable to radiation-induced damage. "He can do simple errands if not pushed," we wrote on his examination records. He was born with an abnormally small head and body size.

In the 1980s, Dr. Masanori Otake and Dr. Schull established specific levels of radiation associated with the grave abnormalities. They found a direct relationship between impaired mental ability, the age of the individual at the time of exposure, and the intensity of the radiation, and they related the level of the radiation dose to severe mental retardation, the frequency of seizures, and general intellectual development. Again and again, work in the laboratory and analyses of clinical observations have confirmed that immature cells, particularly those of the developing brain, are the most vulnerable to radiation damage.

The year 1966 was for me a milestone. At last we were allowed to move some of the research beyond the limits of the laboratory to the direct service of humanity. Two things of special meaning to me occurred. First, the American Academy of Pediatrics convened a three-day conference on the significance of fallout for children, bringing into the discussion citizens' groups, environmentalists, and government officials as well as pediatricians and radiology specialists. Second, the academy magazine, *Pediatrics*, published a survey of laboratory investigations of radiation impact on the brain, suggesting some broad standards of tolerable dosage, a work I had prepared for the academy.

The conference had the effect of bringing into the open the issue of fallout in a way that encouraged the public to seize the initiative in seeking limits on nuclear testing. The magazine survey provided many radiologists with their first detailed information regarding appropriate levels of radiation as indicated by laboratory experimentation. No one had yet proposed precise radiation dosages based on clinical experience, so this was just a preliminary step in helping doctors evaluate the risks in the event radiation was required during a pregnancy or with children.

If nothing else, research at that time attracted attention to the risks in radiation. One obvious preventive step would have been to end the environmental radiation created by weapons testing, and this was a key element of the academy's fallout conference agenda. As we now know all too well, even the underground tests were subject to radiation leakage, and these continued, to say nothing of the tests in the atmosphere. But the governments of the United States, the Soviet Union, and China put up strong resistance to testing limits.

We were also beginning to learn a great deal about fallout.

The apparent absence of lethal consequences from the fallout created by the Hiroshima and Nagasaki bombs was due to the relatively high altitude at which the bombs had been detonated. The explosions did not sweep up in the mushroom cloud vast quantities

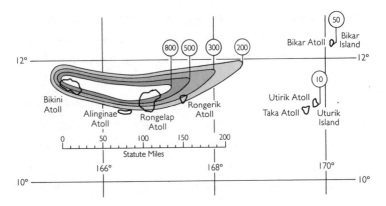

Fallout spread east from Bikini Atoll with diminishing radioactivity. Figures show the dosage in roentgens received by unshielded persons over a period of forty-eight hours. Courtesy of the U.S. Atomic Energy Commission.

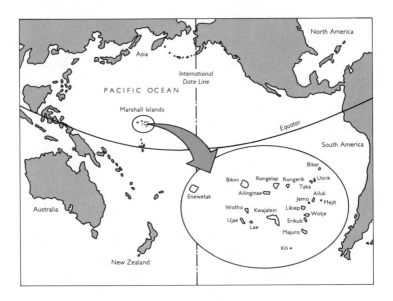

Courtesy of Brookhaven National Laboratory, 1992.

of soil, sand, and water. The so-called black rain that fell in the Nishiyama Valley east of Nagasaki and in the suburbs of Hiroshima caused no serious consequences as far as we now know, and persistent follow-up investigations have continued to confirm the absence of abnormalities. That research has made a major contribution to the whole process of trying to measure precisely the levels of radiation from the bombs at different places and distances.

The Marshall Islands test of a thermonuclear weapon could not have been more different. There was a burst of unprecedented power in that explosion, equal to 15 million tons of TNT, compared with the 22,000-ton equivalent in the Nagasaki bomb. And the Marshall Islands bomb detonated nearer the surface, so that large quantities of earth, sand, and water were admixed and fused with the radioactive fission products.

The intense heat lofted this cloud of lethal materials high above the surface, forming a cloud more than 120 miles long and 30 miles wide. As the cloud cooled, much of the radioactive contents returned to earth as a powdery shroud. The fallout particles clung to the skin of people exposed to the powdery "rain." The fallout was inhaled as people breathed and ingested when they ate contaminated food. Particles in the environment and on the skin of the people emitted gamma rays, which penetrated their bodies, and beta rays, which burned their skin.

The fallout threat was unexpected. American servicemen on Rongerik Island were routinely monitoring for signs of radioactivity when, during an appalling period of thirty minutes, just seven hours after the blast, the telemetering instruments went off the scale. The monitors sounded a "Mayday" to the task force.

The largest and most exposed population was on Rongelap Island, some one hundred miles east of the bomb test site at Bikini. Rescue ships did not arrive there until forty-nine hours after the test explosion. The last person was evacuated fifty-four hours after the fallout reached the ground.

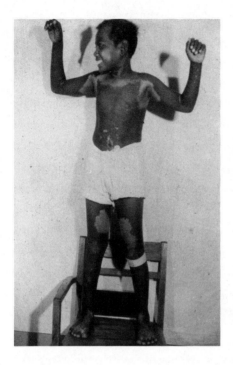

Fallout from the thermo-nuclear bomb detonated by the United States in the Marshall Islands in 1954 had both immediate and long-term effects on the inhabitants. Photo shows extensive radiation burns on a young boy from Rongelap. By permission of Ambassador William F. Kendall, Embassy of the Republic of the Marshall Islands, the U.S. Department of Energy, and the Brookhaven National Laboratory.

"What went wrong?" Dr. Robert A. Conard, one of the leading American medical authorities on the Marshall Islands radiation, asked in his report. "In reviewing the events that occurred soon after the accident, I think that the state of confusion was responsible for the chronology of events that occurred. Certainly no ulterior motive is evident."

By the time the islanders had been evacuated, some had absorbed a radiation dose of as much as 190 rads, four times the average dosage of Nagasaki survivors who had been within a mile and a quarter of the hypocenter. A more prolonged exposure could have resulted in almost immediate death. Nevertheless, a variety of serious clinical consequences occurred.

There was radiation sickness, with transient nausea, vomiting, and diarrhea, although not at a level of seriousness that required special treatment. There were skin burns, loss of hair, and conjunctivitis related to deposits of the fallout on the skin and in the eyes. Abnormal depression of blood elements persisted for several months, although blood counts were normal by the end of a year.

Only a few of the less than 250 persons exposed to the fallout were children, but I was not surprised to find that they suffered the most.

World attention was focused on the fallout problem two weeks after the bomb test when the *Fukuryu Maru — Lucky Dragon* — with a crew of twenty-three Japanese fishermen aboard, docked in Japan with crew members reporting radiation sickness. One died subsequently, although the role of the radiation exposure in his death was not clear. The fishermen had been eighty miles from the test site on Bikini and were exposed to concentrated fallout. Their plight drew attention for the first time to global environmental factors, including the risk of ocean pollution.[23] And for the Japanese, the horrors of Hiroshima and Nagasaki were reawakened along with fears that the nation's vital fish resources were threatened by radioactive contamination.

Reexamination of the Marshall Islands populations has continued in the years since 1986, when the Republic of the Marshall Islands was created under a compact of free association with the United States. That continuation is fortunate, because we can at least benefit from that terrible accident by extending our knowledge of the effects of fallout.

I had been invited to go to the Marshall Islands by Dr. Wataru Sutow, a veteran of the work at Hiroshima. Unfortunately, I could not get away from the heavy load of my practice and research in Los Angeles, but I arranged to receive direct reports from Dr. Sutow and Dr. Robert Conard. Dr. Conard led the group from the Brookhaven National Laboratory for the first twenty-three years of those vital examinations. Their reports became an important element of our committee work at the academy.

In the first decade after the 1954 test, Dr. Sutow reported to me significant evidence of retarded growth in children who had been under five years old at the time of the exposure, with the retardation most marked among those who had been less than eighteen months old.

In the second decade, the researchers were able to relate the growth retardation to lowered function of the thyroid. Thyroid tumors, albeit nonmalignant, were widespread. Clearly thyroid function had been impaired by the children's exposure to the penetrating radiation of fallout particles and the ingested radioiodine that accumulated in their developing thyroid glands.

As time passed, the researchers identified reduced thyroid function, thyroid tumors, or both in almost all of the children who had been under ten years old at the time of exposure to the fallout. One of them, one year old when exposed, had died of leukemia at the age of nineteen. Another developed thyroid cancer.

Two of the three children who were in their mothers' wombs when exposed to the fallout radiation on Rongelap Island showed abnormalities. One had a small head—just as we had observed in Nagasaki—and developed a benign thyroid tumor later. The other developed a thyroid tumor but had a normal head size.[24]

The extent of the hazard of radioiodine absorbed by the thyroid became apparent only after a decade of study. The work also confirmed the high risk of mental retardation among children born with impaired thyroid function unless they received thyroid hormone therapy. Once again, research was demonstrating how vulnerable the human fetus and children are to radiation.

Dr. Schull and I collaborated on an article summarizing these findings for the *Journal of the American Medical Association* in August 1990, titled "Perinatal Loss and Neurological Abnormalities among Children of the Atomic Bomb—Nagasaki and Hiroshima Revisited, 1949–1989." It served, I felt, as an important reminder of what those first bombs had done.

A remarkable new research tool had been developed by the 1980s to permit accurate estimates of the actual radiation dosage received by individuals. The result was DS86, a dosimetry system developed in 1986 to cover most of the survivors. In Japan, scientists used measurements of gamma ray and neutron radiation in the ground, in steel reinforcing rods, in virtually every object exposed to the bomb to calculate the specific level of radiation exposure at each given place. These data were then used to establish a correlation between the medical effect of the bomb on survivors and the precise level of radiation received at a given location. The work was extended in the United States, where weapons testing observations were combined with research at Los Alamos National Laboratory to re-create the atomic bomb effects.

"What about cancer?" was a question asked over and over as we pushed ahead with our research. We were not surprised to find leukemia as the first cancer diagnosed among bomb survivors. There had been a long history of leukemia cases associated with radiation, notably among radiologists. But there were to be some most unexpected findings as the cancer work proceeded.

The discovery of leukemia among the survivors set the stage for what would become the largest cancer research program of its type in the history of medicine. By 1957, more than 100,000 people in Nagasaki and Hiroshima were participating in the program.

When the study began, the emphasis was on using death statistics to calculate the medical consequences of the bombs. But it soon became clear that this would not yield a full and complete answer. Because of modern treatments and other factors, it was likely that many with radiation-induced cancer might survive and eventually die of other causes. So a lifetime study of the incidence of cancer among the survivors was proposed by the ABCC.[25] Each case of cancer was recorded at the time of diagnosis. Hospital records were monitored. Complete tumor registries were established in Nagasaki and Hiroshima. And the actual radiation exposure for each person in the study was calculated using the DS86 dosimetry, providing accurate estimates according to the individual's distance from the hypocenter and any shielding that might have modified the exposure.

The first comprehensive report on the incidence of cancer among the survivors was issued in February 1994, and it covered an extraordinary base of eighty thousand persons. Building on the continuing mortality study, the research confirmed and quantified with new precision the cancer risks of radiation.

Stomach cancer is the most common form of cancer in Japan. The study found 2,658 cases of stomach cancer in the Hiroshima and Nagasaki populations, but only 6.5 percent of the cases were attributed to the effects of radiation. That result contrasts with findings that bomb radiation was a factor in 32 percent of the 529 cases of breast cancer, 26 percent of the thyroid cancer cases, and 24 percent of the skin cancer cases, excluding melanoma.

Clearly, the incidence of cancer resulting from exposure to bomb radiation is not large in total numbers. There had been hints of that while I was in Nagasaki for the first time, and it was confirmed by later studies. But small as the total numbers are, they nevertheless demonstrate a remarkable increase and, above all, serve as yet another measure of the vulnerability of children.

The first case of leukemia attributed to the atomic bombs was diagnosed in Hiroshima in 1951, six years after the bombing, by Dr. Takuso Yamawaki. Dr. Borges, the ABCC hematologist in Hiroshima, and Dr. Jerrett Foley, an internist, joined the research program at Hiroshima and confirmed an unusually high rate of leukemia among the survivors.

At about the same time, we diagnosed two leukemia cases in Nagasaki in a group of sixty-five surviving children who had been among those closest to the hypocenter. A hematologist from the visiting AEC committee came to confirm the diagnosis. We knew that even two cases were significant.

The experiences in both Nagasaki and Hiroshima confirmed the leukemia risk in radiation. Leukemia reached its peak incidence six and seven years after the bombs. The frequency was far greater among children, for this is the malignancy most common to the young. Among children under ten years of age who had been within 1,650 yards of the hypocenter, the incidence was eighteen times higher than for the population as a whole. Among young people ten to nineteen years of age, in the same proximity to the bomb, the incidence was eight times that for the total population exposed to moderate radiation.

Another phenomenon also became apparent. The incidence of leukemia peaked in children much sooner after the exposure than it did in older persons. The incidence among those under fifteen peaked four to eight years after exposure, while for those forty-five and older, the peak incidence came twenty to twenty-two years later.

The 1994 cumulative study found 290 cases of leukemia along with 229 cases of lymphoma and 73 cases of multiple myeloma. The death rate from leukemia among bomb survivors was thirty times its normal level.

Although leukemia was the first cancer to be detected among survivors, breast cancer proved to be more prevalent in the long run, with a total of 529 cases, 32 percent of them attributed to the radiation effect of the bombs. I had the benefit of meeting in Kagoshima with Dr. Masayoshi Tokunaga, who has done the principal work on breast cancer.

"Japan is different," I had been admonished when I began the breast cancer study. The statistics on breast cancer have to be understood against the background fact that Japan has one of the lowest rates of breast cancer in the world.

As with leukemia, the risk of breast cancer was greatest among the young. Those who had been under ten years of age when exposed had a risk five times greater than those forty and older.

The female breast is "the single organ most sensitive to cancer induction after exposure to ionizing radiation," our study concluded. Furthermore, it can now be added that, in young girls, the cells destined to become breast tissue later in life are even more sensitive to cancer induction by radiation than more mature cells. These findings about the vulnerability of immature breast cells echo what we learned in the UCLA research about radiation effects on the developing brain.

We still cannot measure with assurance the extent of late-developing cancers among the survivors. However, the 1994 cumulative report on the incidence of cancer and the ongoing mortality study have demonstrated increases attributable to bomb radiation in the incidence of nine different cancers: breast, colon, lung and respiratory tract, ovary, salivary gland, skin (excluding melanoma), stomach, thyroid, and urinary bladder. At the same time, the study found no increase due to radiation in cancer of the cervix, esophagus, gall bladder, kidney, larynx, oral cavity, pancreas, pharynx, prostate, rectum, and uterus.

In the span of two generations, we have come to know many, perhaps most, of the short-term risks of radiation. Children are the most at risk, particularly for mental retardation, retarded development, and elevated incidence of cancer.

As I planned my return to Nagasaki in 1989, I felt substantial satisfaction in the progress made during the past forty years in understanding the short-term effects and some of the delayed effects of radiation among the survivors. But all of us who participated in the radiation research were perplexed about the absence of a clearer understanding of the genetic impact.

We must wait another twenty years, I think, until the end of the normal life span of the youngest survivors, before we can know the full story of the effects on those exposed to the radiation of the bombs. No one can say how much longer it might take for defects to show up in succeeding generations.

The pain of the uncertainty about genetic effects would be brought home to me on my return to Nagasaki, when I visited the Survivors Consultation Center. I realized then that our work will not be done until we find the genetic legacy of the bombs.

In front of me was the modern Tredia Hotel. Behind me was the re-born city of Nagasaki, surging with life, overflowing with prosperity. Where was the bomb's damage? Where were the acres of twisted and blackened steel frames I had left almost forty years before? I felt as if I were Urashima Taro, the Rip Van Winkle of Japan, as children in the costumes of the Kunchi Fall Festival pranced past me, just as they had done when I first came here.

The children I had known in 1949 as desperate survivors were now middle aged, some of them the parents of these very children I saw moving to a drumbeat along the Nakagawa River bank.

Perhaps I should not have been so disoriented. Aki and I had come back once before, in 1984, but only for a few hours. We had been in China and Korea and our ship stopped briefly in the harbor of Nagasaki. We had time only for lunch with old colleagues, most particularly with Dr. Shirabe, my mentor and my closest colleague in my work as physician in charge of the ABCC. Now, five years after that brief visit, I had counted on a more leisurely opportunity to review with Dr. Shirabe his monumental work, the years he devoted to the victims of the bomb. But I came instead to pay tribute at his memorial service. He had died just months before my return in 1989. He was eighty-nine years old.

This time I came by airplane, landing at the sparkling new airport at nearby Omura, whisked by bus along freeways where we had once struggled across potholes in a Jeep. Fleets of the modern cars of Japan raced with us along the modern highway. I had forgotten how green the countryside is, how verdant the groomed farm plots.

I was already at the Nagasaki Bus Station, hailing a taxi for the hotel, before I realized that I had passed through the Urakami Valley, where I had once stood alone in the wreckage of the vast military-industrial complex destroyed on that August morning in 1945. Only slowly did I begin to recognize landmarks. The Suwa Shrine. The Kaikan Building, our headquarters, a short walking distance from the hotel.

"You were here forty years ago?" I was asked at the hotel, and I knew the clerk wanted to add: "Why now?" Yes, why now? I had come back to try to pull together all that had been found in those forty intervening years:

–about the children who survived,

–about the cancer spawned by the ionizing radiation of the bombs,

–about the deformed children born to pregnant women caught close to the hypocenters of the two bombs,

–and, most perplexing of all, about the genetic effects of the bombs.

Two changes became immediately apparent to me. The Japanese government had elaborated a remarkable support network for the survivors, setting an international standard for research while creating compassionate health services that had not been part of the American occupation. And the impact of the two bombs had inspired a vigorous peace commitment that had not been politically possible in the first years after Japan's defeat in World War II.

The peace commitment was made clear to me at one of my first meetings when I called on Mayor Hitoshi Motoshima. He quickly converted our conversation over tea into a press conference, complete with television crews and reporters from the national newspapers. The mayor cited the work I had done forty years earlier on the human consequences of the bombs to reinforce his call for peace, a crusade he had carried throughout the world.

Three months after I had that visit with the mayor, he was the target of a failed assassination attempt. He had come under bitter attack from ultranationalists in Japan, who particularly resented his criticism of Emperor Hirohito and the emperor's failure to bring the war to an earlier end—before the bombs were dropped.

During Motoshima's tenure as mayor, the Nagasaki Peace Hall was erected in a park on a hill close to the hypocenter. The hall stands next to the International Cultural Center, and together they serve as twin repositories of material on the events of August 9, 1945.

I went there, awed by the photographs that brought back stark memories, moved by the models that depicted the before and after of this particular city, victim of one of the world's two atomic attacks. A million people come each year to this hilltop, half of them schoolchildren, many of them world leaders. No visitor forgets the experience.

The Atomic Bomb Casualty Commission had been reorganized in 1975 as the Radiation Effects Research Foundation (RERF), and it was the leaders of RERF who facilitated my return visits to both Nagasaki and Hiroshima.

The help and hospitality of my old ABCC colleagues were dramatized by a dinner at the Kagetsu, a 350-year-old restaurant famed for its garden as well as its kitchen. Gathered there were many with whom I had worked in 1949, some of them doctors who had made a lifetime commitment to the bomb survivors. We sat discussing this unique and terrifying problem of the twentieth century in an ancient and tranquil setting, a setting that had survived the violence of almost four centuries.

One of the survivors of the bomb, living in Los Angeles, had insisted that I see Tatsuo Setoguchi while I was in Nagasaki. It was good advice. Setoguchi is a broadcast journalist who has been documenting the experiences of thousands of survivors. We met in his office and continued our conversation in a sushi bar. We both felt the contrast as we sat, surrounded by urban normality, talking of the grief of that cataclysmic event that had struck so recently, right here where we sat.

Setoguchi's interviews were conducted many years after the bomb detonated, but he found that the trauma was still raw. For some, he said, just bringing up those events was emotionally overwhelming and they would leave speechless, waiting until another day to continue the interview.

Pervasive among the survivors is a bitterness, a feeling that it was not necessary to bomb a populous area to win the war, he told me. And there is also intractable guilt for many who recall, in the panic of flight, ignoring the cries for help from persons trapped in the rubble, caught under collapsed walls, as fire spread through the shattered city.

"Among the survivors," he continued, "they tell each other they have come this far, but perhaps not many years remain, so that we who have been silent must speak out so that such an event may never happen again to the family of man."

I had shared with the doctors I met in Nagasaki my growing concern about the absence of clear evidence of the genetic effect of the bombs.

"You must visit the Atomic Bomb Survivors Consultation Center," I was told by Dr. Sadahisa Kawamoto, who had been a director of RERF's Nagasaki laboratory. It was a visit that illustrated the importance of finding precise answers to the genetic puzzle.

I had been aware of the local undercurrent of dissatisfaction with the ABCC when I had first served in Nagasaki. Many in the community then thought we should have been providing more health care to the survivors. The ABCC had been largely concerned with studying the medical consequences of the bomb, not with treating its victims.

The Survivors Consultation Center is remarkable both as a model health delivery facility and as an essential element in the search for answers to the genetic riddle. The facility helps the survivors deal not only with discrimination but also with the uncertainty about what the radiation may yet induce in them or their offspring.

"About sixty thousand survivors visit here each year," Dr. Shigeki Toyota, the director, told me. An annual physical examination is offered, and twice-a-year examinations are provided for those who were within two thousand meters of the hypocenter when the bomb detonated. Additional services are offered to those with particular bomb-related health problems. Services are also available at the Atomic Bomb Research Institute at the Medical Center and at the Atomic Bomb Hospital.

I learned, however, of a troubling problem involving the 150,000 *nisei*—the second generation, the children of the survivors. "Very few of the nisei come to the clinic to which they are entitled," Dr. Toyota explained. "It is believed that they may not be anxious to reveal their identity as a nisei whose genetic heritage may be at risk by virtue of their parental exposure to the bomb."

He shook his head.

"We do explain that studies thus far after more than forty years have not revealed any evidence of genetic injury," he went on. "But they are fully aware of the continued efforts that began at ABCC and then at RERF, still searching for findings of genetic injury. So we cannot tell them unequivocally that there is no genetic injury."

The hesitancy of the nisei to reveal themselves leaves a gap in the vast genetic research program that Japan has undertaken. And it increases the uncertainty that touches thousands of lives deeply.

"When a young couple are in love and contemplating marriage they tend to avoid discussing this issue," he added. "Nevertheless, it remains a considerable concern to young couples and their families." And, I was to learn, it remains a considerable concern to the geneticists themselves.

Under the genetic research set up by Dr. Neel, we collected data

on seventy thousand women who had suffered radiation exposure
from the atomic bombs and had become pregnant afterward.[26] The
mothers had sustained radiation ranging from intense to mild. We
examined their children at birth and followed with autopsies of any
who died.

The study of seventy thousand pregnancy outcomes, when completed in 1954, was heralded as "the primary source of information
about the genetic effects of radiation in man." Yet no statistically
valid evidence of genetic damage emerged from this study.

In 1994, five years after my second visit to Japan, I had an opportunity to discuss the genetic riddle in detail with Dr. Neel in his
office at the University of Michigan. Forty-five years had passed since
he had enlisted me in the radiation research while I was completing
my residency at the Children's Hospital of Cincinnati.

Dr. Neel is among those convinced that there has been genetic
damage. He draws a distinction between evidence of damage, which
has appeared in small numbers, and the kind of more widespread
pattern of damage that would be statistically significant.

"We are not saying that there is no effect," he told me during that
visit to his office. "We are being very careful to say that the genetic
risk of radiation is very much smaller than was projected thirty years
ago using mouse experimental data. That should be good news."[27]

Unfortunately, as Dr. Toyota has found in the survivors' clinic, it
is not good enough news to reassure the affected populations. But
Dr. Neel is convinced that the uncertainty will be reduced as better
research tools are developed.

The initial pregnancy outcomes research project sought evidence
of genetic damage by measuring stillbirths, premature births, congenital malformations, birth weight, body measurements, and childhood mortality. Some damage was apparent, but it was limited,
followed no overall pattern, and was not statistically significant.

Seeking significant evidence, the scientists employed a newly developed technique, looking this time for chromosome abnormalities among the survivors. Some damage in the sex chromosomes was found, but again it was not statistically significant. And the same was true when examinations of inherited blood proteins and enzymes were made.

Dr. Neel estimated that the average radiation exposure of the survivors was 40 rads, well below the 300 or more rads that constitute a lethal dose for humans. It was small in comparison with dosages that produced major genetic damage in laboratories, 300–600 rads when mice were studied, 1,000 rads when fruit flies were studied. Apparently, few human beings could absorb a high radiation dose and survive the ferocity of the thermal energy and shock wave of the bombs implicit in greater exposure and closer proximity to the hypocenter.

One way of measuring the genetic effects of radiation is to calculate the so-called doubling dose, the amount of radiation that results in a doubling of the normal incidence of mutations. Dr. Neel calculated that the doubling dose for humans is approximately 200 rads. We can be grateful that the average exposure was only 20 percent of that amount.

"What next?" I asked.

The next step will be an analysis of the DNA in the vast store of blood samples drawn from the survivors. This project will utilize techniques unknown when the genetic study began in 1950.

"This will be the ultimate test," Dr. Neel told me.

The DNA will be analyzed in 1,600 blood samples drawn equally from fathers, mothers, and their offspring.

My last visit to Nagasaki had included a visit to the Atomic Bomb Research Institute and the Tumor and Leukemia Registry at the Medical Center. In the computerized data wing of the institute, detailed records are maintained on 70,000 hibakusha (survivors) who have been treated at the Consultation Center. Specimens from all the patients are maintained in the Tumor and Leukemia Registry. The collection of tissue and blood samples ensures a continuation of the research as new techniques develop.

If the DNA research is no more conclusive than the studies done already, the institute's collection of tissue and blood samples will provide the means to continue the work in the future as even more effective research tools are developed.

"When will the silent bomb within us explode?" one of the survivors commented. But it is not just the hibakusha who need more precise answers about the genetic risks. We all do. For the genetic legacy of nuclear energy is a forever fact.

So I came back to Hiroshima, where the age of atomic warfare had dawned forty-four years before. I came back with my mind crammed with everything I had learned in forty years of intensive study of the effects of the atomic bombs, yet realizing how much more I still needed to know.

I came because Hiroshima, appropriately, is the most important center in the world for research on what the bombs meant in the lives and the deaths of those targeted in August 1945. And I came to talk with the survivors of the first atomic bomb attack, to hear how the years after the bomb had been for them and for their children.

Like the working pediatrician, I was stepping from the laboratory into the examining room. I had read the laboratory reports and the X rays. Now I needed to hear how the patients themselves felt.

When I came for the first time in 1949, I had only a limited opportunity to see Hiroshima. The Hiroshima to which I returned in 1989 was a new city. But it was a city that had wisely retained a stark reminder of its past. The skeleton of a building, part of it stripped to the bare bones of its steel frame by the searing force of the bomb, overlooks Peace Park at the hypocenter.

The RERF keeps its central records in Hiroshima. So I was able to pull together missing elements and confirm other information that tied in with what I had learned in my four decades of studying radiation effects in the United States.

The ongoing research is impressive. The commitment to the highest quality of scientific investigation, perpetuated with both Japanese and American funds, has a special significance in a world in which the risk of nuclear war has not been eliminated. American and Japanese scientists have collaborated, with increasing effectiveness, from the first weeks after the end of World War II. This half century of cooperative work may be without precedent.

Dr. Itsuzo Shigematsu, the chairman of RERF, arranged housing for me in the RERF dormitory at the top of Hijiyama Hill. The facility overlooks the Hiroshima delta where the seven tributaries of the Ota River spread fanlike to the Inland Sea. Adjacent to the dormitory are the foundation's clinic and laboratory. Among the staff welcoming me was Dr. Seymour Abrahamson, chief of research, a geneticist from the University of Wisconsin. From the first morning, Dr. Abrahamson prodded me out of bed at six o'clock for brisk walks through Hijiyama Park in the beautiful autumn weather.

Our guide, whom we knew only as Keiko-san, was one of the survivors, in her teens when the bomb detonated. She brought home to us the horror of her experience one day in a quiet exchange. We had stopped for a snack along the way and I offered her some of the chicken being barbecued over a brazier.

"I have not been able to eat broiled meat since the bomb," she replied. Forty-four years afterward, she could still smell the burning flesh of the dead and dying. Her reaction made more meaningful the cold statistics that more than 130,000 people were killed in Hiroshima, more than 70,000 in Nagasaki.

In the clinics for survivors I was able again to be in contact with those the bomb had most affected. But I was no longer seeing the little boy of five who had been irradiated while in his mother's womb on that August day, whose reduced head size and subnormal mental capacity I had observed in 1951. Now I was seeing the forty-five-year-old, middle-aged and still facing an uncertain future.

From my own pediatric practice I knew well the impact on a family of any abnormality in a child. One of my hardest tasks was telling parents of a deformity or other congenital problem that would change the lives of the entire family. For these families in Hiroshima and Nagasaki, in the aftermath of the bombs, the impact of deformed children was compounded by homelessness, by the deaths of other family members, and by deprivation in the first years after the war.

Where did they get their resilience and courage? I would find one answer when I met with the Mushroom Cloud Auxiliary, the Kinoko-kai. They are the mothers of children scarred for life by the bomb.

"If you want to talk to the mothers of the Kinoko-kai, contact Omuta," Dr. Schull had told me just before I left Los Angeles.

Minoru Omuta, an editor of *Chukoku Shimbun* in Hiroshima, was shocked one day years ago to read of the suicide of a young woman. Her mother had been pregnant with her when exposed to the bomb. The girl had become despondent after reading reports that those exposed to the bomb radiation while in the womb were likely to have abnormalities. She took her own life.

Painstakingly, Omuta began trying to locate the mothers who had been exposed to the bomb's radiation while pregnant. He encouraged them to come together in a support group that came to be called the Mushroom Cloud Auxiliary. Each of the women shares two things: having been close to the hypocenter, and having a child whose life was changed by the bomb.

"Ask the mothers any question you may have, as we may not have another opportunity to meet them because some live at a considerable distance from here and others have to work," Omuta said as we assembled.

Our meeting was in a spacious conference room at the Survivors Health Clinic, part of the Hiroshima Comprehensive Health Center, which offers a full spectrum of diagnostic and treatment services. For me, this health center is a model for all health delivery systems. It integrates the local medical society, state-of-the-art diagnostic and treatment facilities, and the county public health officer, a practicing physician, who is in charge of the center. The capable director is the affable Dr. Chikako Ito, one of a new breed of women physicians in Japan.

I knew something of the group. Several of the women had been scarcely half a mile from the hypocenter. Some had been thrown through the air by the blast and left unconscious. All had suffered radiation illness in some form—lassitude, bloody diarrhea, loss of hair, skin hemorrhaging, ulcerations of the mouth, sores on the face, symptoms that continued for the duration of their pregnancies for some, longer for others.

"Nearly everyone around you must have perished," I commented hesitantly, uncertain how to begin.

There was a chorus of "Hai"—yes, yes. And they rose from their chairs and led me to the window.

"See the Miyuki Bridge below? Up to there, the city was entirely demolished, consumed by the fire. Nothing was left."

And they began their stories.

"My baby was only fifteen hundred grams [3.3 pounds] and was born prematurely at eight months."

"My baby was born at term but weighed only twenty-five hundred grams [5.5 pounds]. I often wondered why I was spared and why even now I am well. You know there were some around us who seemed to have been protected because they had no burns or injury and seemed well at first, and yet within a month or so they were dead."

"I wondered during those days how could the baby inside of me grow, what with the little food we had then. Thin rice gruel was all we had to survive."

When the mothers asked why their children suffered abnormali-

Three hours after the atomic blast, August 6, 1945, Hiroshima. Survivors at the Miyuki bridge just beyond the perimeter of the roaring firestorm two miles from the hypocenter. Some managed to escape to Ujina while others succumbed by the roadside en route. Photograph by Yoshito Matsushige of *Chugoku Shimbun.* Courtesy of *Chugoku Shimbun.*

ties, they were told that it was most likely caused by the malnutrition, trauma, and stress related to the bombing.

"Why didn't they explain to me that it was most likely the radiation that caused such difficulties for the child, when all these years they already had so much information about the radiation harming the fetus? The reexaminations were endless, not realizing that most of us as a single parent could not afford to leave work."

"The problems the child encountered were hardly ever discussed. When the school informed me that they recommended that my child should be enrolled at an institute for children with learning disabilities, I realized how retarded the child was compared with other children. To think that the bomb reached into my womb and hurt him leaves me bitter."

"I lived in the country; so I never went to ABCC. Whenever the child was sick I took him to the family doctor. When he developed seizures, which were frequent, the doctor assured me that it was not epilepsy so he probably would get better as he became older. He treated the convulsions without any reference to the atomic bomb."

They spoke with candor of the problems of being parents of a *Pica* baby, as they are called. *Pica* is the word for "flash," a reference to the blinding light of the bomb.

"Since in the rural districts there were no special facilities to teach children with learning disabilities, she went to school with the other children. Even though some families may have known she was a Pica child, they did not single her out because of it. Classmates took care of her like members of her extended family. They would come after her on their way to school and accompany her home. It was indeed a fortunate situation for our family and our daughter. But later, when reports appeared about how prenatal radiation in Hiroshima and Nagasaki resulted in children with microcephaly and mental retardation, I was aware that some remarks were being made about my daughter. 'She's a Pica baby.' It upset me. But my husband and relatives cautioned me not to confront such individuals and not to discuss my daughter's plight with them. In the future it would hinder the marriageability of the older and younger siblings, they said. So I suppressed my feelings and didn't talk with others about my experience at the time of the bombing."

As I listened, I could sense the strength they gained by coming together as the Mushroom Cloud Auxiliary. I marveled at the quiet way they told their stories. I could only grieve for the uncertainty that still haunts them, the uncertainty of growing older without knowing what might yet be the consequences of the bomb, or who would care for their children, already approaching their fiftieth birthdays, and what might await their children's children.

One mother finally spoke about those concerns. Her husband

had died of cancer. She had already had one operation for stomach cancer. Her daughter was then forty-four.

"Who will look after my daughter when I am gone?" she asked. There was no answer.

Mrs. Kondo did not join the other members of the Mushroom Cloud Auxiliary at that meeting. She wanted to see me alone, to take me out into the city. She insisted. So all other plans for my last afternoon in Hiroshima were canceled.

Kondo is not her real name. Because of her daughter, she prefers that her real name not be published.

When Mrs. Kondo spoke to me in 1989, her daughter was forty-five years old and living far away on Hokkaido in northern Japan. The younger woman suffered the classic symptoms of fetal exposure: microcephaly and mental retardation. With her mother's constant support, she had finished basic schooling, had married, and had borne two children of her own. The children showed no symptoms of abnormality; as in so many other cases, there was no evidence of a genetic effect. But Mrs. Kondo's daughter cannot function as a normal mother in her state of limited mental capability. So she relates to her children much as a sister, and others bear the responsibility of parenthood.

On the day of the bombing, Mrs. Kondo was working with her sister in Hiroshima, barely half a mile from the hypocenter. She was twenty years old and pregnant with her first child. Her husband was teaching that day in a suburb. She had stepped into a narrow alley to wash her hands.

"The moment I bent over the faucet, the strong sunlight of summer vanished and the whole area was enveloped in a pale light," she reported. "I instinctively covered my face with both hands. Then I heard a sound, 'boom.' I raised my head and looked around, but nothing could be seen due to a thick cloud of dust. I slowly found my way to the place where my sister was calling me. The house was flattened. Only one pillar was left, where my sister was standing."

They pulled the landlady from beneath a fallen beam. A young couple, the woman's clothing stripped from her body, both of them covered with blood, held a bleeding baby and pleaded for help to find a second child, lost in the wreckage.

"Then I suddenly noticed that the whole area had caught fire," Mrs. Kondo continued.

She and her sister shielded their bodies with futons and ran down the main street, fires raging on either side, to find refuge with others in a hilltop temple.

"People were groaning with pain, craving water, or asking to be taken home, pleas made with all their remaining strength. I still remember the terrible sight vividly. I was just dumbfounded, wondering how it could have ever happened in the human society, and stood aghast looking over the entire city from the hill all day long.

"The summer sun was blazing over the southern part of the city and the city center was covered with black smoke and fire, which kept shooting up to the sky like a tornado. The place where we were was dark with heavy clouds hanging over our heads. The entire city looked like a hell on earth."

Mrs. Kondo told her own story carefully, but she was more concerned that I understand what had happened to so many of the schoolchildren of Hiroshima when the bomb detonated.

Her car was the smallest I had ever seen, but I managed to crowd into the front seat with her. We drove to one of the landscaped parkways near the hypocenter, parked the car, and began to walk. There were tall stone pieces along the way, decorated with origami paper cranes on strings. The paper cranes this day hung limp and battered from wind and rain.

"These are memorials," she explained.

The children of Hiroshima had been mobilized to clear fire paths and perform other outdoor jobs on that August morning in 1945. Others were standing outside for the traditional morning assemblies. Only a few were inside the school buildings when the bomb deto-

In 1974 survivors submitted drawings and sketches of their memory of the atomic bombing in unexpected response to a request from NHK, Japan's national broadcasting corporation. Many of these drawings, done three decades after the event, were published in *Unforgettable Fire: Pictures Drawn by the Atomic Bomb Survivors*, ed. Japan Broadcasting Corporation (NHK), trans. World Friendship Center in Hiroshima (New York: Pantheon Books, 1977). All are reproduced courtesy of the Hiroshima Peace Culture Foundation.

This drawing shows a view from the Aioi bridge near the hypocenter in Hiroshima on the day after. "I looked toward the Honkawa Elementary School. All of the schoolchildren, who appeared to have been at a morning assembly in the schoolyard, were burned black, squatting in orderly lines, motionless. A relief party was removing the corpses." Kinu Kusata. From *Unforgettable Fire*, p. 65.

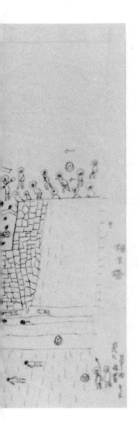

"*Sensei! Sensei! Sensei!* Teacher! Teacher! Teacher!"
A group of schoolgirls seeking shelter, naked and with
strips of burned skin hanging from their outstretched
arms, called out to their teacher near the Koi Elementary School. A sense of responsibility. Kishiro Nagara.
From *Unforgettable Fire*, p. 41.

A mother unable to escape, engulfed in flames, was dead, collapsed on the ground, embracing two children. The childrens' fingers were deeply pressed into the mother's flesh. Akiyama Kazuo. From *Hiroshima* (Tokyo: Doshinsha, 1971), p. 95.

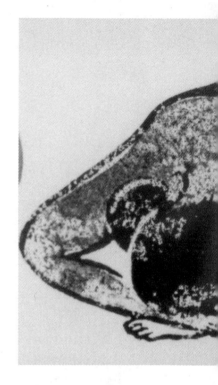

A boy, three to four years old, burned black, points to the sky. Masato Yamashita. From *Unforgettable Fire*, p. 104.

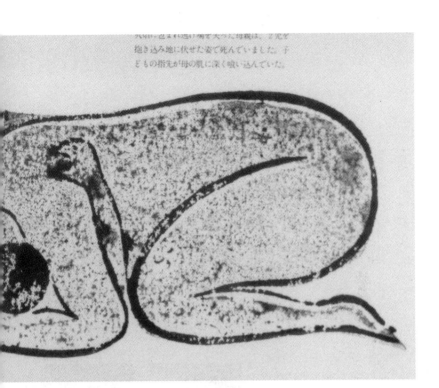

火炎に包まれ逃げ場を失った母親は、２児を
抱き込み地に伏せた姿で死んでいました。子
どもの指先が母の肌に深く喰い込んでいた。

Schoolgirls, scorched and black [later these burns often developed into disfiguring scars]. Tokuoki Hirata. From *Hiroshima* (Tokyo: Doshinsha, 1971), p. 39.

With no one to help her, a girl died by the bank of the Enko River. Masato Yamashita. From *Unforgettable Fire*, p. 103.

"I saw an infant boy leaning against the wall and heard him crying. When I approached and then touched him, I found that he was dead. Just to think that he might have been my son." Name unknown. From *Unforgettable Fire*, p. 54.

Family in flight, "All around us were voices asking for help. We tried to find shelter. Our bodies were covered with blood and choked with the smoke." Ishizu Kazuhiro. From *Hiroshima and Nagasaki: A Pictorial Record of the Atomic Destruction* (Tokyo: Hiroshima-Nagasaki Publishing Committee, 1978), p. 122.

nated. So the death toll of Hiroshima schoolchildren exceeded even that of Nagasaki. Some 84 percent of those unshielded and in the open within four miles of the hypocenter died.

I had heard about the schoolyard situation from Akihiro Takahashi just a day earlier. He was fourteen when the bomb detonated, standing in the playground of his school for morning assembly.

"The all clear had sounded," he recalled. "But I saw a lone plane in the sky. Suddenly, there was an explosive wind, so powerful that it tore off my clothes. And then I felt intense burning."

When he turned his head, I could see only the nub of one ear. That side of his face, and a third of his body, had been literally seared, for he was scarcely a mile from the hypocenter.

"Skin was draped from my arms and body. The exposed flesh was bleeding. I wondered what had happened. Bewildered, I remembered only the drills we had had. Run for the river."

For ten minutes he could do nothing, see nothing. Clouds of debris, smoke, and ash blinded him, darkened the city. When he could see a few yards, he began to run. But he stopped when he heard, "Help me, help me," from a friend. The other boy was in excruciating pain, his legs and the bottoms of his feet burned by the blast.

"So I helped him and we made our way to the Fukushima Bridge. It was shattered but we managed to crawl across remaining beams. We had to pass many bodies, many crying for help. Everything was on fire. We had to keep moving."

He lived, recovering slowly over the next two years, one of eleven survivors in a classroom of sixty. His friend died two weeks later.

To the friend who died, and the others like him in the schoolyards of the city, each Hiroshima school had erected its own stone memorial along this lovely parkway. It was these that Mrs. Kondo was pointing out as we walked.

The names of the dead children are etched in the stone. Four thousand, five hundred names. I had to repeat the number to begin to grasp its dimension. Four thousand, five hundred.

Those memorial stones brought back to me a quiet conversation I had had earlier at the Nagasaki University Medical Center with Dr. Setoguchi. He had brought me the Nagasaki school death reports.

"So here we have Shiroyama Primary School, 500 meters from the hypocenter," he reported. "Let me see. There were 1,324 registered students and 1,284 died. And there is Inasa Primary School. Its children lived 1,000 meters to 2,000 meters from the hypocenter. There were 906 registered at the school; 622 were killed."[28]

Unimaginable figures. A pediatrician inevitably deals with death, but it is the death of a single child, and even then one can see the terrible toll it takes on the family. But here we were speaking of sudden deaths on a scale previously unknown, a disruption of families beyond calculation. Death touched every family in Hiroshima that day.

World War II was indeed a different kind of war. It was different in terms of the immense increase in the power of the weapons used, culminating in the atomic bombs. And it was different in the indiscriminate way these increasingly lethal weapons were used against entire populations, women and children among them.

Whole cities, not just military installations, had become targets. I had seen it myself. I had watched from the Offlag XIII-B camp the Allied bombings of Frankfurt. I had narrowly escaped death in the day-long bombing of Nuremberg as our column of prisoners of war made its way out of the city. I had read of the rocket bombing of London. But nothing had prepared me for the Nagasaki and Hiroshima death tolls. So many children dead and disabled.

My last dinner in Hiroshima was in a sushi bar with Mrs. Kondo, the doctor who had cared for her daughter, and the doctor's wife. Mrs. Kondo drove me back to the RERF dormitory after dinner. As we were saying good-bye, she handed me a piece of paper that was, in effect, her mission in taking me to the memorials to the children of Hiroshima. It was her commitment to work so that what happened in Hiroshima and Nagasaki would never happen again.

"Doctor," she said, "we must protect each other. This is not a problem of tomorrow. We must confront it now for the sake of the future of our children living in the Nuclear Age."

She is right, of course. Yet nothing that has happened in the years since I said good-bye to her has eased my concern about the continuing risk of nuclear war, a risk amplified by the proliferation of nuclear weapons.

When I was speaking to a high school class recently about my experiences, one of the students asked me what I thought about the bomb and nuclear energy.

"Should we have dropped the bomb?"

I learned the brutality of conventional warfare in the Ardennes. I understand the military calculations that must have anticipated an Allied amphibious assault on Japan, the estimates of tens of thousands of American casualties. Many of my medical school classmates were poised at advance bases in Okinawa, the Philippines, and Iwo Jima for the invasion of Japan.[29] They and their families received news of the bomb and the ensuing peace with a sense of unqualified relief.

There may have been other calculations of which I knew, and know, nothing. There are those who are convinced that American leaders knew the collapse of Japan was imminent but unleashed the bombs as the best way to test their effects. There are others who believe that the emperor steadfastly resisted surrender or peace negotiations until after the bombs were dropped.

But I now also know, beyond any doubt or uncertainty, what an atomic bomb can do. I know the measure of its human toll. So I answer the question of the high school student this way:

If they knew then what we know now about what an atomic bomb can do, it would have been the wrong thing to do.

Knowing what we know now, we cannot condone the use of nuclear weapons.

"Radiation is a wonderful and life-saving tool in modern medicine," I recently told a friend, thinking of all the diagnostic and treatment applications that were part of my own pediatrics practice.

Every thought, every judgment is colored, however, by the knowledge of the destructive power of the atom.

As I left Hiroshima the next day, I could not erase the memory of Mrs. Kondo, cut off from her only daughter, a daughter so damaged by the bomb that she can only be a sister to her own children.

I thought of the Marshall Islanders, the people of Rongelap, driven into exile by their own pervasive fear of the power of radiation, and two generations of the people of Bikini who still cannot safely go home.

I thought of the uncertainties that are the inheritance of all the children of the atomic bomb in Japan—

Couples coming together in marriage, bravely concealing their exposure or the exposure of their parents to the bombs, but never able to forget the fear of genetic damage that might be revealed with the birth of a child, or a grandchild, or a great-grandchild.

The hibakusha, often the victims of shocking discrimination, yet patiently participating in the endless research, unwitting sentinels warning the world that the deleterious consequences of an atomic blast extend beyond the instant casualties to lifetimes of uncertainty.

I thought of that little boy, so long ago, whose head size and behavior said so much about the power of a bomb.

And Akihiro Takahashi, the fourteen-year-old in the schoolyard in Hiroshima, who told me, forty-four years later, that he still hears the cry of his friend, "Help me, help me," and the cries of others he could not help.

"Do not forget us, Dr. Yamazaki." That was what Mrs. Kondo said, just before she drove off in her small car.

How could I?

This book is my way of remembering. It flows from my conviction that every decision maker, every citizen, needs to know the human cost of nuclear warfare. I want no mistakes. I want no decisions that ignore the very particular vulnerability of children, and through the children, the vulnerability of the future of all of us.

THE PEACEMAKER

Think not forever of yourselves, O Chiefs
Nor of your own generations.
Think of continuing generations of our families.
Think of our grandchildren and of those yet unborn,
Whose faces are coming from beneath the ground.
—On the formation of the Iroquois Confederation
many centuries ago

APPENDIX

A. Major ABCC/RERF Programs

Program	Number of Subjects	Year Study Initiated
Survivors		
Life span	110,000	1958
Pathology	70,000	1962
Adult health (Biennial examination)	29,000	1958
In utero	2,800	1956
Genetics: Children of survivors		
Pregnancy outcome	76,626	1948–54
Mortality	77,000	1955–69
Cytogenetics	33,000	1969
Biochemical genetics	45,000	1975

B. Comparative Radiation Dose Effect (in millirad = 1/1,000 rad)

Source	Dose Rate	Average Estimated Dose
Natural	per year	100 mrad, whole body
Man-made		
Atomic bomb:		
Survivors, average	~1 minute	40,000 mrad, whole body
Radiation sickness	~1 minute	120,000 mrad, whole body
Lethal dose	~1 minute	400,000 mrad, whole body
Global fallout	per year	4 mrad, whole body
Nuclear power	per year	0.003 mrad, whole body
Chest X ray	<1 minute	<30 mrad, chest
Cigarettes, 1–2 packs/day	per year	8,000–9,000 mrad, lungs

Notes: When the same radiation dose is divided and given over an extended period the effect is reduced. The dose has been adjusted for qualitative difference of various types of radiation.

Sources: Composite sources; see Glossary references.

GLOSSARY

Atomic bomb. A weapon of mass destruction. The term is sometimes taken
to mean a nuclear weapon utilizing fission energy only, but it is ap-
plicable to hydrogen fusion weapons as well. It is appropriate to call
both atomic weapons because the energy released by atomic nuclei is
involved in each case. The energy of an atomic explosion is released in
a number of ways:

–as an explosion qualitatively similar to the blast from a conventional
(chemical-TNT) bomb explosion but thousands of times more powerful;

–as direct instant nuclear radiation consisting of penetrating gamma rays
and neutrons;

–as direct thermal radiation of visible, infrared, and ultraviolet rays;

–as the instant creation of a variety of radioactive particles thrown up into
the air by the force of the blast and extremely high temperature, suck-
ing up dirt and debris from the earth's surface, forming a massive
mushroom-shaped cloud. As the cloud ascends and cools, the radioactive fission products and debris particles condense, returning to earth
as fallout and emitting radiation over a variable period;

–as a sharp pulse of electromagnetic energy (EMP) capable of damaging
unprotected electric and electronic equipment at great distances.

See *Nuclear weapons.*

Atomic Bomb Casualty Commission (ABCC). A commission established in
accordance with a 1946 presidential directive to the National Research
Council (the operations arm of the National Academy of Sciences)
to undertake long-term investigations of the medical and biological
effects of radiation on A-bomb survivors in Hiroshima and Naga-

saki. Japanese participation commenced in 1948 under the auspices
of the Japanese National Institute of Health of the Ministry of Health
and Welfare. The ABCC's funding was initially from the U.S. Atomic
Energy Commission, later supplemented by the National Cancer Institute and the National Institute of Heart and Lung Disease. The ABCC
was succeeded by the Radiation Effects Research Foundation (RERF) in
April 1975.

Atomic Energy Commission (AEC). A civilian agency established by an act of
Congress in 1946 to regulate nuclear weapons development and testing
and develop peaceful uses of atomic energy. Between 1942 and 1946,
before the AEC was established, weapons development and testing were
the responsibility of the Manhattan Engineer District, U.S. Army.

ATB. At the time of the bomb.

Blast wave. A pulse of air whose pressure increases sharply at its front. A
blast wave is initiated by the expansion of the hot gases produced in
an atomic explosion and is accompanied by winds of extremely high
velocity; a suction-negative phase follows, reversing the wind direction.

Cancer. A malignant tumor of potentially unlimited growth, capable of in-
vading surrounding tissue or spreading to other parts of the body by
metastasis.

Carcinoma. A malignant tumor (cancer) of epithelial origin.

Cell culture. The growing of cells *in vitro* in such a manner that the cells are
no longer organized into tissues.

Cohort study (or follow-up study). An epidemiological study in which groups
of people are identified with respect to the presence or absence of exposure to a disease-causing agent and the outcomes in terms of disease
rates are compared.

DNA. Deoxyribonucleic acid; the primary hereditary molecule in most
species. Genes are made of DNA.

DS86 dose. Accurate and precise estimates of the radiation to which A-
bomb survivors were exposed have been developed through the joint
efforts of scientists from Japan and the United States, who measured
radiation doses at weapon tests, reactor simulations, and radiation-
induced changes in materials and the earth in the vicinity of the

detonations in Hiroshima and Nagasaki, and calculated the shielding afforded by structures and terrain. As organs within the body also provide shielding, these effects were also calculated for the major organs of each survivor. Accurate dose determination is essential for evaluating radiation-induced biological effects. The analyses of the major ABCC/RERF studies from 1958 to 1987 have been revised, and a DS86 dose has been determined for each A-bomb survivor. Nearly eighty thousand individuals were involved in the cancer incidence and mortality studies, and seventy thousand individuals in the genetic study.

The cancer incidence and mortality data from Hiroshima and Nagasaki reveal a clear relationship between doses of radiation and ill effects.

Epicenter. The location in space where the atomic bomb exploded (cf. *Hypocenter*).

Epidemiology. The study of the determinants of the frequency of disease in humans. The two main types of epidemiological studies of chronic disease are cohort (or follow-up) studies and case control (retrospective) studies.

Fallout. The process or phenomenon by which radioactive particles are dispersed in the atmosphere following a nuclear explosion and subsequently settle to the earth's surface. Early, or local, fallout is defined, somewhat arbitrarily, as those particles which reach the earth within twenty-four to forty-eight hours after a nuclear explosion. Delayed, or worldwide, fallout consists of the smaller particles that ascend into the troposphere or stratosphere and are carried by winds aloft to all parts of the earth. Delayed fallout returns to earth mainly in rain and snow over extended periods of weeks, months, or years.

The type and amount of fallout vary with the location of the point of burst in relation to the surface of the earth. Following an underwater burst, for example, besides massive local atmospheric fallout, the radioactive debris returns in a downpour, or "rainout," within minutes after the explosion, with considerable environmental consequences to aquatic life; additionally, the surrounding area is shrouded by a lethal radioactive mist.

Firestorm. A massive stationary fire, generally in built-up urban areas, in which strong winds rush inward toward the fire from all sides. The winds keep the fire from spreading outward while adding fresh oxygen to increase its intensity. The firestorm may be lethal even to those sheltered from the flames because of the intensity of the heat and the depletion of the available oxygen; e.g., in Hiroshima and the firebombing of Dresden.

Fission, nuclear. The splitting of a heavy atom accompanied by the emission of neutrons and gamma rays and the liberation of a large amount of energy. The nuclear fragments formed (fission products) are usually radioactive. Nuclear fission is the opposite of nuclear fusion. The most important and readily fissionable weapon materials are uranium 235 and plutonium 239.

Fission products. Highly radioactive fragments produced in the fission of uranium or plutonium nuclei in an atomic explosion. There are eighty or so types of these highly radioactive fragments. When they descend to the earth's surface, fission products constitute fallout.

Furoshiki. A wrapping cloth.

Fusion, nuclear. A nuclear reaction occurring at extremely high temperatures in which nuclei of light atoms, especially those of the isotopes of hydrogen, combine to form a heavier nucleus, accompanied by the liberation of an enormous amount of energy. It is the opposite of nuclear fission. See *Nuclear weapons*.

Hibakusha (atomic bomb survivor). Currently there are over 368,000 survivors in Hiroshima and Nagasaki. They are classified by the following government designations: (a) individuals who incurred physical and medical injury, including children in the womb of injured mothers; (b) those exposed to residual radiation who entered the area near the hypocenter soon after the explosion and those exposed to the fallout (black rain); (c) families whose key members were disabled or killed at the time of the bombing. Special government entitlements are provided for those within 1.2 miles of the hypocenter who were injured or who developed radiation-related illnesses. Data from medical investigation of the delayed effects of radiation show that the risk of developing cancer for survivors who were more than 1.5 miles from the hypocenter is no greater than for those not in the city at the time of the bombing.

Hypocenter. The point on the earth's surface directly beneath the spot where the atomic detonation actually occurred.

Incidence (or incidence rate). The rate of occurrence of a disease within a specified period of time, often expressed as number of cases per 100,000 individuals per year.

In utero. In the womb; i.e., before birth.

In vitro. Literally, "in glass"; in the test tube.

In vivo. In the living organism.

Isotopes. Forms of the same element having identical chemical properties but differing in their atomic masses (because they have different numbers of neutrons in their respective nuclei) and nuclear properties. For example, hydrogen has three isotopes: hydrogen, with a mass of 1; deuterium, with a mass of 2; and tritium, with a mass of 3. The first two are stable (nonradioactive), but tritium is a radioactive isotope. Nuclides have the same number of protons in their nuclei and hence the same atomic number, but differ in the number of neutrons and therefore in mass. Both isotopes of uranium, with masses of 235 and 238 units respectively, are radioactive (emit alpha particles), but their half-lives are different, releasing their radioactivity at a different rate. Furthermore, uranium 235 is readily fissionable by neutrons of all energies, while uranium 238 is not.

Joint Commission for the Investigation of the Effect of the Atomic Bomb in Japan. A commission formed by the Office of the Supreme Commander of the Allied Powers on October 12, 1945, to coordinate the interests of the Manhattan Project Group, the GHQ Group under the Chief Surgeon's Office, the U.S. Navy Medical Corps, and the Japanese government.

Latent period. The period of time between exposure to a disease and expression of the disease. After exposure to a massive dose of radiation, for example, there is a delay of several years (the minimum latent period) before any cancers are seen. Leukemia has a shorter latent period than most solid malignant tumors.

Life-span study (LSS). The ongoing study of the Japanese atomic bomb survivors at ABCC/RERF. The base sample of the study consisted of 120,000
people, of whom 82,000 were exposed to radiation from the bombs,
mostly low doses. Subsets of the life-span studies are still being utilized
for ABCC/RERF investigations.

Machi, cho. A district in Japan.

Mortality (rate). The rate at which people die from a disease (e.g., a specific type of cancer), often expressed as number of deaths per 100,000
people per year, or per 10,000 per year.

Mutation. A heritable change in the DNA molecule. Such changes in the
genetic material result in new inherited variations that are usually
harmful to their possessors. Mutation occurs naturally and may also be
caused by ionizing radiation and other physical and chemical agents.

National Academy of Sciences–National Research Council (NAS-NRC). The
academy is a private, nonprofit society of scholars established by Congress in 1863 to advise the federal government on scientific and technical matters. The council was organized by the academy in 1916
and serves as its principal operating agency. Members of the National
Academy of Engineering and the Institute of Medicine are also now
participants of the NAS-NRC.

Neoplasm. Any new and abnormal growth, such as a tumor. A neoplastic
disease is any disease that forms tumors, whether malignant or benign.

Nuclear weapons (or bombs). A general name given to weapons that use
energy released by reactions involving atomic nuclei—either fission or
fusion or both. The atomic bomb and the hydrogen bomb are both
nuclear weapons, since the energy of atomic nuclei is released in each
case. It has become more or less customary, although it is not strictly
accurate, to refer to weapons in which all the energy results from atomic
fission as A-bombs or atomic bombs. In order to make a distinction,
weapons whose energy results at least in part from the thermonuclear
(fusion) reaction of the isotopes of hydrogen have been called H-bombs
or hydrogen bombs.

Prevalence. The number of cases of a disease in existence at a given time
per unit of population, usually 100,000 but sometimes per 10,000.

Radiation, background or natural. The amount of ionizing radiation to which a member of the population is exposed from natural sources, such as terrestrial radiation due to naturally occurring radionuclides in the soil, cosmic radiation originating in outer space, and naturally occurring radionuclides deposited in the human body.

Radiation, doubling dose. The amount of radiation needed to double the natural incidence of a genetic or somatic anomaly.

Radiation Effects Research Foundation (RERF). A binationally funded Japanese foundation chartered under Japanese law according to an agreement between the United States and Japan. The RERF is the successor to the ABCC (Atomic Bomb Casualty Commission).

Radiation, electromagnetic. A traveling wave produced by oscillating magnetic and electric fields. Electromagnetic radiation ranges from X rays (and gamma rays), of short wavelength and high frequency; through the ultraviolet, visible, and infrared regions; to radio waves of relatively long wavelengths (low frequency). All electromagnetic radiation travels at the speed of light — 186,000 miles per second.

Radiation, ionizing. Any electromagnetic radiation or particulate radiation capable of displacing electrons from atoms or molecules, directly or indirectly, in its passage through matter, namely, X-ray and gamma radiation; or particulate radiation, including alpha radiation (alpha particles = helium nuclei), beta radiation (negative- or positive-charged electrons), and neutrons. Ionizing radiation causes instant biochemical changes within and around cells, reflected in both acute symptoms and delayed effects. Depending on the dose, the injury may be repaired or may cause cell death and death of the organism.

From a weapons standpoint, ionizing radiation occurs as (a) invisible penetrating gamma rays and neutrons released at the instant of the atomic explosion; and (b) radioactive fission fragments of a wide variety of elements that return to the earth as fallout, emitting gamma rays and beta particles over an extended period. See *Radioactivity.*

Radiation, principal types.

Alpha particles or streams of particles, called *alpha rays*, are emitted spontaneously from the nuclei of some radioactive elements. Each alpha particle is identical to a helium nucleus having a mass of 4 units and an electric charge of 2 positive units (see *Radioactivity*). Alpha particles produce intense ionization along their path and have relatively low penetrating power—less than 0.1 mm in tissue. They enter the body through inhalation or ingestion and exert their effect at the point of exposure. The well-known watch dial painters, who painted the dials with luminescent radium, ingested the radium, which emitted alpha particles that destroyed bone tissue and caused cancer of the bone. Uranium and plutonium that escape fission may be ingested or inhaled and may emit alpha particles, a potential source of injury.

A *beta particle* is an electron or in some cases a positron ejected from a nucleus of a radioactive nuclide. *Beta rays* are streams of beta particles. Their ionizing power is far less than that of alpha rays, but their penetrating power is greater. Their range in tissue (which varies with the energy of beta particles) is rarely more than 2 cm; e.g., skin burn from fallout particles that adhered to the skin. Ingested radioactive iodine, which emits beta rays (and also gamma rays), is capable of destroying thyroid tissue in larger doses, especially in very young subjects, and producing thyroid tumors and cancer.

Gamma radiation (or gamma rays) is short-wavelength electromagnetic radiation of nuclear origins that penetrates matter, similar to X rays but usually of higher energy; X rays are produced by processes outside the atomic nucleus. Radium emits gamma rays and, in minute amounts, is utilized in the treatment of localized cancer.

Neutrons are neutral particles present in all atomic nuclei except those of ordinary hydrogen. Neutrons are required to initiate the fission process, which in turn produces a large number of neutrons. Neutrons are produced by both fission and fusion reactions in nuclear (atomic) explosions. Neutrons and gamma radiation produced the direct instant radiation casualties in Hiroshima and Nagasaki.

Radiation sickness. The complex of symptoms characterizing excessive exposure of the whole body (or a large part) to ionizing radiation. The earliest symptoms are nausea, fatigue, vomiting, and diarrhea, which may be followed by loss of hair, hemorrhage, inflammation of the mouth and throat, and loss of energy. Instant death follows a massive dose of radiation. In severe cases, death may follow within hours, days, or weeks. Those who survive six weeks after the receipt of a single large dose of radiation may be expected to recover. The major long-term effect among the survivors is cancer. Individual variability to toxic substances, including ionizing radiation, is recognized clinically and experimentally. As with all toxic substances, there is considerable variation in response to a given exposure dose of radiation.

Radiation, thermal. Electromagnetic radiation emitted from the fireball of an atomic explosion as a consequence of its very high temperature; it consists essentially of visible light, ultraviolet, and infrared radiation. The absorption of this energy by the air results in the formation of the fireball. Approximately a third of an atomic bomb's energy is released as thermal radiation. In brightness a nuclear detonation is comparable to the sun.

Radiation, units of measurement.

Roentgen (r). A unit that measures the exposure dose of X-ray or gamma radiation.

Rad (roentgen absorbed dose). The absorbed dose of any ionizing radiation imparted to matter by ionizing particles or electromagnetic radiation per unit mass of irradiated material is expressed in rads or grays; 100 rads = 1 gray (Gy, the si unit); e.g., a "routine" chest X ray exposes the patient to 0.05 r = 0.05 rad = 0.05 centiGy. The exposure dose may be attenuated by other body structures, structural materials, and terrain surrounding a target so that the absorbed dose may be fractionally lower. [See appendix table comparing radiation doses.]

Curie. The quantity of radioactive material, evaluated according to its radioactivity; now replaced by *Becquerel* (Bq), the si unit of activity.

SI units. The International System of Units as defined by the General Conference of Weights and Measures in 1960. These are generally based on the meter/kilogram/second units; special quantities for radiation include the Becqueral, Gray, and Sievert.

Radioactivity. A natural or artificially induced process consisting of electromagnetic or particle radiation from an atomic nucleus.

Radioactivity, artificial. Man-made radioactivity produced by fission, fusion, particle bombardment, or electromagnetic irradiation; e.g., radioactive fallout produced by fission of uranium and plutonium emits gamma radiation and alpha and beta particles.

Radioactivity, natural. The property of radioactivity exhibited by more than fifty naturally occurring radionuclides; e.g., uranium 238 and radium emit gamma rays and alpha and beta particles. The entire population of the world is exposed to natural radioactivity, and always has been.

Shielding. Any material or obstruction, including terrain, that absorbs radiation and thus tends to protect personnel from the effects of atomic explosion. A moderately thick layer of any opaque material will provide satisfactory shielding from thermal radiation, but a considerable thickness of high-density material — e.g., lead — may be needed for protection from nuclear radiation. Concrete and water absorb the energy of gamma rays and neutrons.

UNSCEAR. United Nations Scientific Committee on the Effects of Radiation. The committee publishes periodic reports on the sources and effects of ionizing radiation.

X rays. Electromagnetic radiation identical to gamma rays but produced by processes outside the atomic nucleus.

Sources

Butler, Clay B. "The Light of the Atom Bomb." *Science* 138 (1962): 483–89.

Committee on the Biological Effects of Ionizing Radiation, Board on Radiation Effects, Research Commission on Life Sciences, National Research Council. *Health Effects of Exposure to Low Levels of Ionizing Radiation (BEIR V)*. National Academy Press, Washington, D.C., 1990.

The Effects of Nuclear War. U.S. Congress, Office of Technology Assessment, Washington, D.C., 1979.

The Effects on Population of Exposure to Low Levels of Ionizing Radiation. Report of the Advisory Committee on the Biological Effects of Ionizing Radiations, Division of Medical Sciences, National Research Council. National Academy of Sciences, Washington, D.C., 1972.

Evans, G. D. "Cigarette Smoke = Radiation Hazard." *Pediatrics* 92 (September 1993): 464.

Glasstone, S., and P. Dolan, eds. *The Effects of Nuclear Weapons.* Third edition. U.S. Department of Defense and U.S. Department of Energy, Washington, D.C., 1977.

Hearings Before the Subcommittee on Research, Development, and Radiation on Radiation Standards and Fallout. Joint Committee on Atomic Energy. 87th Cong., 2d sess., June 1962. Part 1, pp. 3–14.

Lean, Geoffrey, ed. *Radiation Doses, Effects, Risks.* United Nations Environment Programme, Nairobi, Kenya, 1985.

Lindell, Bo, and Lowry Dobson. *Ionizing Radiation and Health.* World Health Organization, Geneva, 1961.

"Review of Forty-five Year Study of Hiroshima and Nagasaki Atomic Bomb Survivors." *Journal of Radiation Research* 32, suppl. 1 (1991): 1–412.

Solomon, Frederic, and Robert Q. Marston, eds. *The Medical Implications of Nuclear War.* Institute of Medicine, National Academy of Sciences. National Academy Press, Washington, D.C., 1986.

Stannard, J. Newel. *Radioactivity and Health: A History.* Ed. R. W. Baalman, Jr. Prepared by the Pacific Northwest Laboratory for the U.S. Department of Energy. Office of Scientific and Technical Information, Springfield, Va., 1988.

Tsuzuki, Masao, ed. *Medical Report on Atomic Bomb Effects.* Medical Section, Special Committee for the Investigation of the Effects of the Atomic Bomb, National Research Council of Japan, January 1947. [Eight other sections reported on the biological, environmental, and physical effects of the atomic bomb. This report was the first publication of the medical consequences of the atomic bomb. The investigations began soon after the bombing, and the early findings were incorporated into the joint commission's reports in 1951 and 1954.]

U.S.-Japan Joint Workshop for Reassessment of Atomic Bomb Radiation Dosimetry in Hiroshima and Nagasaki, Japan, February 16–17, 1983. Radiation Effects Research Foundation, Hiroshima, Japan.

NOTES

1   This feeling was pervasive in Hiroshima and Nagasaki and still persists nearly five decades later. Yet, a large segment of the survivors in Hiroshima and Nagasaki have participated in the ABCC/RERF investigations with the cooperation of the medical institutions of both cities. Prior to the formal surrender of Japan and before the Allied occupation forces had arrived in Japan, one of the first memoranda concerning the investigation of the atomic bomb effects expressed this perspective: "A study of the effects of the two atomic bombs used in Japan is of vital importance to our country. This unique opportunity may not again be offered until another world war" (A. W. Oughterson et al., "Medical Effects of the Atomic Bomb," in *Report of the Joint Commission on the Effects of the Atomic Bomb in Japan,* vol. 1, app. 1, p. 24 [U.S. Atomic Energy Commission, Technical Information Service, Oak Ridge, Tenn., 1951]).

    Once it was generally recognized that an atomic bomb had caused the destruction, the leading physicians of Japan immediately began to investigate the medical implications of the weapon. See the comment by Dr. John Bugher, deputy director of the Division of Biology and Medicine, Atomic Energy Commission, about the interest of the Nagasaki Medical School faculty in continuing to observe the long-term effects among the survivors, in note 20.

2   This is the document requested by the War Department in February 1942. Without it, my commission, dated November 25, 1941, could have been revoked. Consulate of Japan, Los Angeles, Calif.: "In accordance with the National Citizenship Law, Section 20, Article 3, Paragraph 2, the [Japanese] citizenship of the persons named hereafter has been cancelled on the 12th day of the 10th month of 8th year of Showa Era (October 12, 1933) and the notice thereof has been published in the official Bulletin 329 of the Department of Home Affairs: Yamazaki Tamio (Peter), Yamazaki Michio (John), Yamazaki Nobuo (James). Translation, certified correct and made by R. J. Mittewer, Notary Public for the County of Los Angeles, February 6, 1942, and recorded in the County Recorder's Office."

3   Executive Order 9066, issued by President Franklin D. Roosevelt, authorized
    the secretary of war and the military commander to exclude all aliens and citi-
    zens to provide security in designated areas. On April 22, 1942, the following
    announcement was delivered and posted widely in Uptown: "EXCLUSION ORDER
    NO. 11. WESTERN DEFENSE COMMAND, FOURTH ARMY, INSTRUCTION TO ALL PERSONS OF
    JAPANESE ANCESTRY. PROHIBITED AREA."

4   On December 18, 1944, the Supreme Court confirmed the criminal conviction
    of Fred Korematsu for violating Western Defense Command Civilian Exclusion
    Order No. 34 (based on President Roosevelt's Executive Order 9066) because
    he had refused to report for evacuation. He contended that he had reported for
    induction, thus signifying his intention to serve in the armed forces of the United
    States. Meanwhile, many Niseis already in the armed forces were summarily dis-
    charged and often reclassified as unfit for military service by their draft boards;
    they were then summarily disenfranchised.

    Nearly four decades later, in January 1983, a legal effort was initiated to re-
    verse the 1944 conviction of Fred Korematsu that was confirmed by the Supreme
    Court. This effort was based on recently discovered documents from government
    files disclosing that government lawyers both suppressed and altered evidence
    submitted to the Justices in the Korematsu internment case. A provision of an
    obscure and little-used provision of federal law (Permission for Writ of Error
    Corum Nobis) permits criminal defendants who have exhausted all their ap-
    peals and who have served their sentences to reopen their case. As ruled by the
    Supreme Court, the only ground for such a proceeding is that the original trial
    was tainted by "fundamental error" or that the conviction resulted in "manifest
    injustice" to the defendant.

    On November 10, 1983, when handing down the opinion of the U.S. District
    Court for the Northern District of California, Judge Marilyn Hall Patel found
    "substantial support in the record that the government deliberately omitted rele-
    vant information and provided misleading information" to the Supreme Court.
    "The judicial process is seriously impaired," she concluded, "when the govern-
    ment's law enforcement officers violate their ethical obligations to the court,"
    and she vacated Korematsu's wartime conviction. Never before had any judge va-
    cated a criminal conviction upheld by the Supreme Court on a final appeal. Peter
    Irons, ed., *Justice Delayed: The Record of the Japanese American Internment
    Cases* (Middletown, Conn.: Wesleyan University Press, 1989), pp. 125–249.

5   At the annual beer bust of the Sepulveda Men's Golf Club at the Coors brewery
    in Van Nuys in 1989, a mutual friend introduced me to Dale Gustafson, formerly

of the 28th Infantry Division, as a fellow "Kriege" (*Krieggefangene*, prisoner of war). We met later, and his account suggested that he was in the same railroad marshalling yard in Hanover when we were bombed: "The sirens were pulsating at about 30 seconds, then there was hardly any pause. It felt [like] the bombs' explosions would pick up the boxcar and then slam us down again and again. Dead ducks. Our own planes going over us. Scary."

6   Letter from Committee of Atomic Casualties, National Research Council, March 9, 1948, signed by Herman Wigodsky: "Study and evaluation of children will be a major part of the project effort.... It is the belief of the committee that the project will remain in Japan for ten years and we hope for at least 50 years."

7   The principal U.S. government groups of the Joint Commission studying atomic bomb effects in Japan, and later, separate reports by the Manhattan Engineering Project, the Atomic Energy Commission, and the Atomic Bomb Casualty Commission all recognized the invaluable support of Dr. Tsuzuki, who served as the principal liaison with the Japanese government in providing information about the casualties in Hiroshima and Nagasaki. His understanding of the biological effects of radiation was based on experiments at the University of Pennsylvania in the early 1920s, the results of which were reported in the article "Experimental Studies on the Biological Action of Hard Roentgen Rays," *American Journal of Roentgenology and Radium Therapy* 16 (1925): 134–50. His familiarity with English also facilitated the investigations shared between the American and Japanese groups.

8   Masao Tsuzuki, *Medical Report on Atomic Bomb Effects* (Medical Section, Special Committee for the Effects of the Atomic Bomb, National Research Council of Japan, January 1947). This is the first medical report of the initial findings of the medical investigations in Hiroshima and Nagasaki. In the United States it is available only in special collections. The findings have been mostly incorporated into the *Report of the Joint Commission on the Medical Effects of the Atomic Bomb in Japan*, U.S. Atomic Energy Commission, 1951–54. I obtained this report in 1989 from Dr. Tsuzuki's son, who was chairman of the Department of Surgery at Tokyo University.

9   British Commonwealth Occupation Forces, Headquarters QG/801/2/Accm., March 5, 1949. Subject: *Use of BCOF Facilities by U.S. Personnel* (distribution included the director of the ABCC). "Paragraph 2: Japanese nationals or persons of Japanese extraction, except when the latter are wearing the uniform of the United States Armed Forces, and except as stated in paragraph 6 below, cannot be permitted to enter or use any BCOF facility (e.g., bus service, housing, schools,

etc.). Signed, D. G. McKenzie, Lt.-Col., for Brigadier, Principal Administrative Officer."

10 Quotations from the S. L. Warren Papers, 987, Box 63, Special Collections Library, UCLA. "Secret" classification canceled June 7, 1965: "Selected group of officers and enlisted men Manhattan Engineering District sent to Japan to investigate A Bomb effects. Group under the immediate command of Colonel Stafford L. Warren. The group is composed of physicians, physicists, radiologists, chemists, engineers. Ordered by the War Department to measure radioactivity, number and type of casualties: Clinical records, histories, autopsies. Preliminary examination early September, followed by surveys 20 September to 12 October 1945."

In a letter to Gavin Hardin, Armed Forces Project: "I shall never forget walking into the medical school in Nagasaki about 8 weeks after the detonation . . . stepping over the body of a young female partly burned, going down the corridors of an American designed concrete building like those at home, finding in room after room laboratory equipment so familiar at home and on the floor two or three bodies. They must have been doctors, nurses, technicians, and students. Outside was a pile of bones of cremated bodies. Pile was about three feet deep and fifty feet in diameter."

11 Atomic Bomb Investigation, Memorandum to Major General Groves, War Department, United States, Engineering Office, New York, N.Y., November 27, 1945. 1. Preliminary Report of the Technical Service Detachment in Japan from 5 September 1945 until 12 October 1945: Section I: Medical report; Section II: Radioactivity measurements; Section III: Damage estimates; a copy of the eyewitness report of Father Siemens, S.J., in a report to the Pope (copy obtained).

12 James N. Yamazaki, Nagasaki Atomic Bomb Casualty Commission Quarterly Report, 1 January 1950–31 March 1950, p. 9, subject: residual radioactivity investigation by William Menker and Leon Levinthal, Tracer Laboratory chemists, for ten days beginning the first week of March. Their investigation was centered in the Nishiyama Valley and the reservoir, which served as a catch basin for rain-washed fission products.

13 For days and weeks after the explosion, measurements were taken of residual radiation from neutrons and gamma rays in the area close to the hypocenter and of the fallout from fission fragments in more distant areas (E. T. Arakawa, "Radiation Dosimetry in Hiroshima and Nagasaki Atomic Bomb Survivors," *New England Journal of Medicine* 263 (1960): 488–93). Persistent fallout from fission products contributed additional irradiation in a few locations where there

was significant initial fallout; the amount of initial fallout could be estimated provided that storms or runoffs had not washed away a large portion of it. In the months after the bombing, U.S. medical and armed forces groups substantiated earlier findings (Stafford L. Warren, "The Role of Radiology in the Development of the Atomic Bomb," in *Radiology in World War II*, ed. Kenneth D. A. Allen [Washington, D.C., 1966]; Nello Pace and Robert E. Smith, *Measurement of the Residual Radiation Intensity at the Hiroshima and Nagasaki Atomic Bomb Sites* [Bethesda, Md.: National Naval Medical Center, 1959], pp. 1–29). In the ensuing decades, U.S. and Japanese collaborative efforts have continued to assess the effects of radiation. Newer methods of mensuration (e.g., the DS86 dosimetry system) further verified earlier findings that the dosage of residual radioactivity was relatively small and that the direct instant radiation from the bomb caused both the early and late biological effects. In its recent thorough review, the "Black Rain" Committee in Hiroshima also confirmed previous findings (Itsuzo Shigematsu, letter to author, 22 February 1995). The committee added that the radiation dosage from black rain did not directly cause an increased rate of death among the survivors.

Induced radioactivity near the hypocenter has been estimated at 18 to 24 rads for Nagasaki and about 50 rads for Hiroshima. The cumulative maximal dose from fallout has been estimated to be as low as 3 rads in the Koi and Takasu areas of Hiroshima but as high as 30 rads in the Nishiyama district of Nagasaki (Shunzo Okajima, Shoichiro Fujita, and John H. Harley, "Radiation Doses from Residual Radioactivity," in *U.S. Japan Joint Reassessment of Atomic Bomb Radiation Dosimetry in Hiroshima and Nagasaki, Final Report: DS86 Dosimetry System*, vol. 1, pp. 223–24 [Hiroshima: Radiation Effects Research Foundation, 1986]). The only documented finding of early or late effects was a transient elevation of the white cell count in residents of Nishiyama in the months after the explosion. By comparison, the Marshallese on Rongelap atoll were exposed to 190 rads of fallout in the two days before their evacuation. In addition, the internal dose from ingested radioiodine deposited in the thyroid was considerably greater than 190 rads, later producing significant injury to that organ. However, life-threatening symptoms did not develop from this external and internal radiation at the time of exposure.

14   S. J. Kimura's 1950 Nagasaki cataract survey was filed with the ABCC in Hiroshima and was incorporated into subsequent surveys in Nagasaki.

15   In conjunction with this study we undertook a study with Drs. M. Setoguchi and A. Takao (designated ABCC OP Ped 46) of 134 children under the age of nineteen,

survivors who had been within 1,000 meters of the hypocenter. These patients were reexamined again in the spring of 1951 when Drs. S. Wright and P. Wright joined the study. Two individuals among these 134 children were diagnosed with leukemia at the time of the second examination. The observations are included in J. Folley et al., "Incidence of Leukemia in Survivors of the Atomic Bomb in Hiroshima and Nagasaki," *American Journal of Medicine* (September 1952).

16   Case Summary, Treatment and Disposition to Glen Line, Limited. Re: Captain's Steward Ho Lung Yue, aboard MV *Glenarm*. Head, neck, chest steel fragment wounds incurred in air attack at sea. 17 July 1950, Nagasaki Harbor. Signed, J. Yamazaki, M.D., Atomic Bomb Casualty Commission.

17   Interviews with Hitoshi Tokai and Toshiko Murakami. Both were teenage students mobilized to work at the Mitsubishi ordnance factory three quarters of a mile from the hypocenter. Photograph on p. 91, taken the day after the bombing, shows the Matsuyama district that Hitoshi crossed to reach his home.

18   Members of the AEC Advisory Committee for Division of Biology and Medicine, Drs. Merril Eisenbud and Ernest Goodpasture, visited Nagasaki in January 1951. On their return to Washington they recommended that the ABCC project be terminated. U.S. Atomic Energy Commission, Minutes of the Advisory Committee for Biology and Medicine, January 12–13, 1951. From Merril Eisenbud, *An Environmental Odyssey: People, Pollution, and Politics in the Life of a Practical Scientist* (Seattle: University of Washington Press, 1990), pp. 110–12, 147.

19   AEC consultants visited Nagasaki in May 1951 led by Dr. John C. Bugher, deputy director of the Division of Biology and Medicine, with Drs. Wilbur Davison of Duke University, John Lawrence, and William Vallentine of UCLA. They made a thorough evaluation of the administrative, personnel, community relationship, and scientific aspects of the Nagasaki ABCC.

20   Dr. Bugher personally encouraged further development of the working relationship with members of the faculty: "There is at Nagasaki the oldest medical school in Japan, and one of the most respected. Despite the catastrophe which befell this school in which the major portion of the faculty and student body met death there is a determined and effective effort underway to re-establish this institution, even without help from outside. Here are people available, intensely interested and also eager to develop their own facilities in any manner which offers reasonable and hopeful prospect." The participation of the physicians from the medical school became an integral part of the Nagasaki ABCC project.

21   The need to disseminate the rapidly accumulating information on radiation's particular hazard to children was recognized and brought to the attention of the

American Academy of Pediatrics by a few informed pediatricians, among them Doctors Robert Aldrich, first director of the National Institute of Child Health and Development; Lee Farr, chairman of the Committee on Atomic Casualties, National Academy of Sciences, National Research Council; Paul Wehrle, later president of the academy; Robert W. Miller, chief of epidemiology at the National Cancer Institute, who had served in the Hiroshima ABCC; and Fred Silverman, radiologist at the Children's Hospital of Cincinnati. They provided the leadership for the committee, eventually named the Committee on Environmental Hazard.

22   Guidelines for radiation protection are formulated by the International Commission on Radiological Protection (ICRP), and in the United States by the National Council on Radiation Protection and Measurements (NCRP), created in 1929. These groups periodically review information on the risks of radiation exposure to set the standards for radiation exposure. E.g., see NCRP, *Basic Radiation Protection Criteria* (National Council on Radiation Protection and Measurements, report no. 39, 1971).

23   In 1956 a congressional joint committee on the general subject of long-term radiation hazards was formed with personnel from the military and peacetime atomic energy programs. The Special Subcommittee on Radiation began hearings on the nature of radioactive fallout and its effects in 1957. Government and academic experts testified during several sessions through 1963. Part 1 of the hearings, "The Nature of Radioactive Fallout and Its Effect on Man," took place in May 1957. Part 2, a continuation, took place in June 1957. In June 1959, four years after the accidental exposure of the Marshallese to radioactive fallout, the hearings were directed to a session on "Biological and Environmental Effects of Nuclear War." The purpose of this hearing was to clarify for the public the difference between the worldwide fallout from nuclear weapons tests and fallout that would result from the use of these weapons in an all-out war. The problem considered the hypothetical use of 3,950-megaton (3,950,000,000 tons) total yield within one day. Classified military information was not presented.

24   W. W. Sutow, personal communication, October 29, 1979, regarding prenatally exposed Marshallese children.

25   See the appendix table summarizing major ABCC/RERF programs.

26   See James V. Neel and William J. Schull, *The Children of Atomic Bomb Survivors: A Genetic Study* (National Academy Press, Washington, D.C., 1991). Planning for the genetic program began in 1946, and data have been collected continuously since 1948. This 518-page anthology includes the results of the principal

investigations undertaken by the authors and their resident Japanese colleagues in Hiroshima and Nagasaki at the ABCC and RERF laboratories. It is the most extensive genetic epidemiology ever undertaken.

27   Interview with J. V. Neel, University of Michigan, Ann Arbor, May 9, 1994.

28   "Report of Student Casualties in Hiroshima by the First Tokyo Army Hospital, November 1945." A tabulation of students, the name and location of their schools, and their occupation at the instant of the detonation, compiled by teachers and parents, noted the following: of 6,226 students documented in the report within 1.2 miles of the hypocenter, 4,825 perished. The original reports are in the Stafford Warren Papers, 987, Box 61, Folder 1, Special Collections Library,

In 1974, when NHK, Japan's national broadcasting corporation, requested survivors of the atomic bomb to submit drawings of what they recalled about their experience in 1945, an unexpected number of responses followed. These poignant drawings drew so much attention that they were published in a book, *Unforgettable Fire*. Even after three decades, several drawings reflect the survivors' deeply etched memories of what happened to their children. A few of these illustrations were selected for our narrative.

29   When the atom bombs were dropped on Hiroshima and Nagasaki, my old classmates from UCLA and Marquette University Medical School were in the U.S. Army, Navy, and Marine units poised and alerted for the invasion of Japan. Mituso Usui, a lifelong friend, was a paratrooper with the U.S. Military Intelligence Service on Okinawa. Bill Hiroshima was with MacArthur's headquarters in the Philippines. From the class of 1943 at Marquette was Ed Turich, on the USS *Morgan*, who met my roommate, Edward Lau, on the shores of Okinawa caring for our casualties. George Collentine survived the wave that went ashore from the USS *Sanborn* just one hour after the assault at Iwo Jima began. In the Philippine Islands, Bob Fox was attached to a general hospital being readied to care for the high casualties anticipated from the invasion of Japan. John Conway was on a destroyer off Kyushu when it was disabled by a kamikaze attack. Robert Aldrich, who was with the Fleet Marine Force Amphibious Corps on a rocket launcher vessel-LCIR, expressed the universal thought of the combatants after Iwo Jima and Okinawa: "[We were] acutely aware of the campaigns that would lie ahead. Suddenly the war ended as it had begun, with an unbelievable surprise, the atom bomb. My thankfulness for this cannot be overstated in view of what we expected to be asked to do in the next few months." I worked with Bob in the American Academy of Pediatrics when he was the chair of our committee on radiation effects.

REFERENCES

Prologue

Yamazaki, James N. "Atomic Bomb Casualty Commission—Nagasaki. Current Status and Discussions of the Pediatric Projects in Nagasaki." Proceedings of Meetings of the Research Committees of Hiroshima and Nagasaki, ABCC, June 4, 1951.

1 Nagasaki

ABCC. Nagasaki Memoranda re: Dr. James N. Yamazaki, Meetings with Governor Sugiyama, 13 February 1950; Mr. Deguchi, Chief of Police, 20 February 1950; and Mrs. T. Murakami, President of Midwives Assn., 21 February 1950.

Bowers, John Z. *Western Medical Pioneers in Feudal Japan.* The Josiah Macy, Jr., Foundation. Baltimore: Johns Hopkins University Press, 1970.

Fulop-Miller, René. *The Jesuits: A History of the Society of Jesus,* trans. F. S. Flint and D. P. Tait. New York: Capricorn Books, 1963.

Manhattan Engineering District. "The Atomic Bombings of Hiroshima and Nagasaki." Los Alamos Historical Museum, Los Alamos, N.M., 1946. (M) 4440d. 77.373 Library (M).

Nagasaki 100: '89 Nagasaki Municipal Centennial. Nagasaki City, 1989.

Okamoto, Yoshitomo. *The Namban Art of Japan: The Heibonsha Survey of Japanese Art,* trans. Ronald K. Jones. English ed.: New York: John Weatherhill; Tokyo: Heibonsha, 1972. Japanese ed.: *Namban Bijutsu,* 1965.

Oughterson, A. W., et al. "Medical Effects of the Atomic Bomb." In *Report of the Joint Commission on the Effects of the Atomic Bomb in Japan,* vol. 1, app. 1, p. 24. U.S. Atomic Energy Commission, Technical Information Service, Oak Ridge, Tenn., 1951.

Reischauer, Edwin O. *The Japanese.* Cambridge, Mass.: Harvard University Press, 1978.

2   Born in America

Bosworth, Allen R. *America's Concentration Camps.* New York: W. W. Norton, 1967.

Chuman, Frank F. *The Bamboo People: The Law and Japanese Americans.* Chicago: The Japanese American Citizens League, 1981.

Conrat, Masie, and Richard Conrat. *Executive Order 9066: The Internment of 110,000 Japanese Americans.* Los Angeles: California Historical Society, 1972.

Dower, John W. *War without Mercy: Race and Power in the Pacific War.* New York: Pantheon Books, 1986.

Ichioka, Yuji. *The Issei: The World of the First Generation Japanese Immigrant, 1885–1924.* New York: Free Press, 1988. [See chapter 6, "Struggles against Exclusion"; chapter 7, "The 1924 Immigration Act."]

Kennedy, John F. *A Nation of Immigrants.* New York: Harper and Row, 1964.

Okubo, Mine. *Citizen 13660.* New York: Columbia University Press, 1946.

The Pacific War and Peace: Americans of Japanese Ancestry in Military Intelligence, 1941 to 1952. San Francisco: Military Intelligence Service Association of Northern California and the Japanese American Historical Society, 1982.

Tanaka, Chester. *Go for Broke: A Pictorial History of the 100/442 Regimental Combat Team.* Richmond, Calif.: Go for Broke, Inc., 1982.

Toland, John. *The Rising Sun: The Decline and Fall of the Japanese Empire.* New York: Random House, 1970.

The View from Within. Japanese American Art from the Internment Camps, 1942–1945. Japanese-American National Museum, UCLA Wright Art Gallery, UCLA Asian American Studies Center, 1992.

3   Pearl Harbor's Impact

Churchill, Winston S., and the Editors of Life Magazine. *The Second World War*, vols. 1 and 2. New York: Time, Inc., 1959.

Cook, Haruko Taya, and Theodore F. Cook. *Japan at War: An Oral History.* New York: New Press, 1993. [Interviews of actual participants, military and civilians, abroad and at home.]

Elliot, Gil. *Twentieth Century Book of the Dead.* New York: Charles Scribner's Sons, 1972.

Okihiro, Gary Y. *Cane Fires: The Anti Japanese Movement in Hawaii, 1865–1945.* Philadelphia: Temple University Press, 1991.

Pearl Harbor: December 7, 1941–December 7, 1991. Life Collector's Edition, Fall 1991.

Sulzberger, C. L. *World War II.* New York: American Heritage, 1966.

Toland, John. *The Rising Sun: The Decline and Fall of the Japanese Empire.* New York: Random House, 1970.

World War II. Time-Life Books History of the Second World War. New York: Prentice-Hall, 1989.

4 Love and War in 1944

Baron, Richard, Abraham Baum, and Richard Goldhurst. *Raid: The Untold Story of Patton's Secret Mission.* New York: G. P. Putnam, 1981.

Dupuy, R. Ernest. *St. Vith Lion in the Way: The 106th Infantry Division in World War II.* Washington, D.C.: Washington Infantry Journal Press, 1949.

Eisenhower, John S. D. *The Bitter Woods.* New York: G. P. Putnam, 1969.

Kline, John, ed. *The Cub of the Golden Lion Passes in Review (106th Infantry Division).* St. Paul: West Publishing, 1981.

MacDonald, Charles. *A Time for Trumpets: The Untold Story of the Battle of the Bulge.* New York: William Morrow, 1985.

Patton, Robert H. *The Pattons: A Personal History of an American Family.* New York: Crown Publishers, 1994. [The Hammelburg raid is discussed on pp. 269–70.]

Peterson, Richard. *Healing the Child Warrior (WW II American POWs).* Cardiff by the Sea, Calif.: Consultors, Inc., 1992.

Shaffer, Ronald. *Wings of Judgment: American Bombing in World War II.* New York: Oxford University Press, 1985.

Sherry, Michael S. *The Rise of American Air Power: The Creation of Armageddon.* New Haven: Yale University Press, 1987.

5 Homecoming and the Bomb

"Genetic Effects of the Atomic Bombs in Hiroshima and Nagasaki." *Science* 106 (1947): 331–32. Based on the Genetic Conference, Committee on Atomic Casualties, National Research Council, June 24, 1947. [J. V. Neel presents his plan for the genetic study in Japan.]

Goldstein, L., and D. P. Murphy. "Microcephalic Idiocy Following Radium Therapy for Uterine Cancer during Pregnancy." *American Journal of Obstetrics and Gynecology* 18 (1929): 189–95.

Gregg, N. M. "Congenital Defects Following Maternal Rubella (German Measles) during Pregnancy." *Medical Journal of Australia* 2 (1945): 122.

Warkany, Joseph. *Congenital Malformations, Notes and Comments.* Chicago: Year Book Medical Publishers, 1971.

Warkany, J., and E. Schraffenberger. "Congenital Malformations Induced in Rats by Roentgen Rays." *American Journal of Roentgenology and Radium Therapy* 103 (1947): 520.

Warren, Stafford. *An Exceptional Man for Exceptional Challenges,* vols. 1 and 2. Oral History Program. Regents of the University of California, 1983.

Warren, Stafford L. "The Role of Radiology in the Development of the Atomic Bomb." In *Radiology in World War II,* ed. Kenneth D. A. Allen, a volume in the series Medical Department of the U.S. Army in World War II. Washington, D.C.: U.S. Surgeon-General's Office, 1966.

6 To Japan at Last

Tsuzuki, Masao. *Medical Report on Atomic Bomb Effects.* Medical Section, Special Committee for the Investigation of the Effects of the Atomic Bomb, National Research Council of Japan, January 1947 (translated into English, 1953).

7 Getting Organized

Braw, Monica. *The Atomic Bomb Suppressed: American Censorship in Japan 1945– 1949.* Lund Studies in International History, ed. Goran Rystad and Sven Tagil. Malmo, Sweden: Liber Forlag, 1986. Originally a Ph.D. dissertation, Lund University, Sweden.

Committee for the Compilation of Materials on Damage Caused by the Atomic Bomb in Hiroshima and Nagasaki. *Hiroshima and Nagasaki: The Physical, Medical, and Social Effects of the Atomic Bombings.* Trans. Eisei Ishikawa and David L. Swain. New York: Basic Books, 1981. Originally published in Japanese. Tokyo: Iwanami Shoten, 1979. [For suppression of news relating to the A-bomb and press code invoked by SCAP, see pp. 14, 497, 508.]

Oughterson, Ashley W., George V. LeRoy, Averil A. Liebow, E. Cuyler Hammond, Henry L. Barnett, Jack D. Rosenbaum, and B. Aubrey Schneider. *Medical Effects of the Atomic Bomb in Japan,* 6 vols. Vol. 6 declassified on December 28, 1954. Washington, D.C.: U.S. Atomic Energy Commission, 1951. Limited distribution.

Oughterson, Ashley W., and Warren Shields. *Medical Effects of the Atomic Bomb in Japan*. New York: McGraw-Hill, 1956. [Based on the above six-volume report.]

Shirabe, Raisuke. "My Experience of the Nagasaki Atomic Bombings: An Outline of the Damages Caused by the Explosion." Presented at the Nagasaki University Medical School at his eighty-seventh birthday celebration, May 17, 1986.

Shirabe, Raisuke. "Medical Survey of Atomic Bomb Casualties (Nagasaki)," ed. W. S. Adams, S. W. Wright, and J. N. Yamazaki. *Military Surgeon* 113 (1953): 250. [A more detailed handwritten version of this report was given to RERF by Dr. Shirabe's family and translated into English.]

Smyth, Henry DeWolff. *Atomic Energy for Military Purposes: The Official Report on the Development of the Atomic Bomb under the Auspices of the United States Government, 1940–1945*. Stanford: Stanford University Press, 1989. Originally published by the U.S. government in 1945.

Symposium by the Survivors of the Nagasaki Medical College, Relating Their Personal Experiences with the Atomic Bomb Victims in Nagasaki. Held June 7, 1950, at the Nagasaki Medical College with participation of the ABCC members, chaired by Raisuke Shirabe, Professor of Surgery, edited by James Yamazaki.

8   The Thunderbolt

Akizuki, Tatsuichiro. *Nagasaki 1945*. Trans. K. Nagata, ed. G. Honeycombe. Quartet Books, London, 1981.

The Atomic Bomb: Voices from Hiroshima, ed. Kyoko Shelden and Mark Shelden. Armonk, N.Y.: M. E. Sharpe, 1989. [A collection on the nuclear holocaust expressed by the survivors as well as some of Japan's most distinguished writers and artists.]

Committee for the Compilation of Materials on Damage Caused by the Atomic Bombs in Hiroshima and Nagasaki. *The Impact of the A-Bomb, Hiroshima and Nagasaki, 1945–85*. Trans. Eisei Ishikawa and David L. Swain. Tokyo: Iwanami Shoten, 1985.

Committee of Japanese Citizens to Send Gift Copies of a Photographic and Pictorial Record of the Atomic Bombings to Our Children and Fellow Human Beings of the World. *Hiroshima and Nagasaki. A Pictorial Record of the Atomic Destruction*. Tokyo: Hiroshima-Nagasaki Publishing Co., 1978. [This publication illustrates the vivid aftermath of the atomic bombing.]

The Crazy Iris and Other Stories of the Atomic Aftermath, ed. and introduced by Kenzaburo Oe. New York: Grove Press, 1985. Originally published as *Atomic*

Aftermath: Short Stories about Hiroshima and Nagasaki. Tokyo: Shueisha Press, 1984.

Groves, Leslie R. *Now It Can Be Told: The Story of the Manhattan Project.* New York: Da Capo Press, 1970.

Gladstone, Samuel and Philip J. Dolan, eds. *The Effects of Nuclear Weapons.* Washington, D.C.: U.S. Department of Defense and Department of Energy, 1977. [Coverage from 1950 to 1977.]

Hachiya, Michihiko. *Hiroshima Diary: The Journal of a Japanese Physician, August 6– September 30, 1945.* Trans. and ed. Warner Wells. Chapel Hill: University of North Carolina Press, 1955.

Hersey, John "Hiroshima." *New Yorker,* November 1946.

Ibuse, Masui. *Black Rain,* trans. John Bester. Tokyo: Kodansha International, 1969.

Japan Broadcasting Corporation (NHK), ed. *Unforgettable Fire: Pictures Drawn by the Atomic Bomb Survivors.* English translation by World Friendship Center in Hiroshima, supervised by Howard Schonberger and Leona Row. New York: Pantheon Books, 1977.

Lifton, Robert Jay. *Death in Life: Survivors of Hiroshima.* New York: Simon and Schuster, 1967.

Manhattan Engineering District. "The Atomic Bombings of Hiroshima and Nagasaki." Los Alamos Historical Museum, California, 1946. (M) 4440d. 77.333 Library (M). [See "The Attacks—Nagasaki" on p. 9.]

The Meaning of Survival: Hiroshima's 36 Year Commitment to Peace. Edited and published by Chugoku Shinbun and the Hiroshima International Cultural Foundation. Hiroshima, 1983.

Oe, Kenzaburo. *Hiroshima Notes.* Ed. David L. Swain, trans. Toshi Yonezawa. Tokyo: YMCA Press, 1981. Originally published in Japan as *Hiroshima Noto.*

Pacific War Research Society. *The Day Man Lost Hiroshima, 6 August 1945.* 1972. Tokyo: Kodansha International, 1989.

Shiotsuki, Masao. *Doctor at Nagasaki: "My First Assignment Was Mercy Killing."* Trans. Simul International. First English ed. Tokyo: Kosei Publishing Co., 1987.

9   Expanding Research

Arakawa, E. T. "Radiation Dosimetry in Hiroshima and Nagasaki Atomic Bomb Survivors." *New England Journal of Medicine* 263 (1960): 488–93. [Cites the early radiation measurements taken in Hiroshima and Nagasaki soon after the atomic explosion; data from the Reports on the Investigation of the Atomic Bomb Disasters, Japan Science Promotion Society, 1953.]

Berg, Samuel. "History of the First Survey on the Medical Effects of Radioactive Fallout (Nishiyama Valley, Nagasaki, 1945)." *Military Medicine* (November 1959): 782–85.

Cogan, D. G., S. F. Martin, and S. J. Kimura. "Atomic Bomb Cataracts." *Science* 119 (1949): 654–55.

Cogan, D. G., S. F. Martin, S. J. Kimura, and H. Ikui. "Ophthalmologic Survey of Atomic Bomb Survivors in Japan, 1949." *Transcripts of the American Ophthalmologic Society* 48 (1950): 62. [Atom bomb-caused cataracts.]

Filmore, P. "Medical Examination of Hiroshima Patients with Radiation Cataracts." *Science* 116 (1952): 332–33.

Goulden, Joseph C. *Korea: The Untold Story of the War.* New York: Times Books, 1982.

Hansen, Wayne R., and John C. Rodgers. "Radiological Survey and Evaluation of Fallout Area from the Trinity Test: Chupadera Mesa and White Sands Missile Range, New Mexico." Los Alamos National Laboratory, Los Alamos, N.M., 1985. LA 10256, MS UC11.

Ibuse, Masuji. *Black Rain.* Trans. John Bester. Tokyo: Kodansha International, 1969.

Kimura, S. J., and H. Ikui. "Atomic Bomb Cataracts: Case Report with Histopathological Study." *American Journal of Ophthalmology* 34 (1951): 811.

Lansing, Lamont. *Day of Trinity.* New York: Atheneum, 1965.

Nakaidzumi, Masanori (Tokyo), and K. Shinohara (Nagasaki). "Problems of Contamination of the Bombed Area. Radioactivity of the Atomic Bomb from the Medical Point of View. Fission Fragments in the Nishiyama District, Nagasaki." In *Medical Report on Atomic Bomb Effects*, pp. 32–37, 81–89. Medical Section, Special Committee for the Investigation of the Effects of the Atomic Bomb, National Research Council of Japan, January 1947.

Neel, J. V., W. J. Schull, D. J. McDonald, N. E. Morton, M. Kodani, K. Takeshima, R. C. Anderson, W. Wood, R. Brewer, S. Wright, J. Yamazaki, M. Suzuki, and S. Kitamura. "The Effect of Exposure to the Atomic Bombs on Pregnancy Termination in Hiroshima and Nagasaki, Preliminary Report." *Science* 118 (1953): 537–41.

Okajima, Shunzo, Shoichiro Fujita, and John H. Harley. "Radiation Doses from Residual Radioactivity." In *U.S.-Japan Joint Reassessment of Atomic Bomb Radiation Dosimetry in Hiroshima and Nagasaki, Final Report: DS86 Dosimetry System*, ed. W. C. Roesch, vol. 1, pp. 205–26. Hiroshima: Radiation Effects Research Foundation, 1986.

Pace, Nello, and Robert E. Smith. *Measurement of the Residual Radiation Intensity at the Hiroshima and Nagasaki Atomic Bomb Sites*, pp. 1–29. Bethesda, Md.: Naval Medical Institute, National Naval Medical Center, 1959. [Measurements made 70 to 100 days after the explosion.]

Shigematsu, Itsuzo. Chairman, Radiation Effects Research Foundation, Hiroshima, Japan. Letter to author, 22 February 1995.

Stannard, J. Newell. *Radioactivity and Health, a History*, ed. Raymond W. Baalman. Springfield, Va.: National Technical Information Service, 1988.

Szasz, Ferenc Morton. *The Day the Sun Rose Twice: The Story of the Nuclear Explosion July 16, 1945*. Albuquerque: University of New Mexico Press, 1984. [See chap. 6, "The Aftermath I: Fallout."]

Tessmer, Carl F., and Daniel Brown. "Carcinoma of the Skin in Bovine Exposed to Radioactive Fallout." *Journal of the American Medical Association* 170 (1962): 210–14. [A report of an animal exposed to radioactive fallout on the range near Alamogordo in July 1945 following the detonation of the first atomic bomb at the Trinity test site.]

10   Through Guileless Eyes

Glynn, Paul. *A Song for Nagasaki*. Grand Rapids, Mich.: William B. Erdmans Publishing Co., 1988.

Nagai, Takashi. *The Bells of Nagasaki*. Trans. William Johnson. Tokyo: Kodansha International, 1984. Originally published as *Nagasak no kane*. Tokyo: Hibiya Shuppan, 1949.

Nagasaki Appeal Committee. *Living beneath the Atomic Cloud: The Testimony of the Children of Nagasaki*. Ed. Takashi Nagai, comp. Frank Zenisek, trans. Volunteer Citizens Group of Nagasaki. English ed.: Wilmington, Ohio: Wilmington College, 1983. Originally published in 1949.

Nakazawa, Keiji. *Barefoot Gen: The Day After. A Cartoon Story of Hiroshima*. Trans. Dadakai and Project Gen. Philadelphia: New Society Publishers, 1987. [First serialized in 1972–73 as *Hadashi no Gen* (Barefoot Gen) in Shukan Shonen Jampu, the largest weekly comic magazine in Japan.]

Osada, Arata. *Genbaku no-Ko-Hiroshima no Shonen Shojo no utae* [Children of the atomic bomb—testament of the boys and girls of Hiroshima]. Japanese ed.: Tokyo: Iwanami Shoten, 1951. English ed.: Tokyo: Uchida Rokakuho; and New York: G. P. Putnam, 1959. [Memoirs of the orphaned children.]

Setoguchi, M. "Effects of Atomic Bomb on Children." *Nika Shinryo* [Journal of Pediatrics Praxis] 14 (1951): 167.

11 Lobbying and Researching

Bugher, John C. "Report on the Atomic Bomb Casualty Commission Field Operation March–May 1951," p. 26 and appendixes. Report to Atomic Energy Commission, Washington, D.C., 1951. [Recommends continuing the fundamental program for both Hiroshima and Nagasaki.]

Committee on Radiation Hazards and Epidemiology of Malformations, American Academy of Pediatrics. "Statement on the Use of Diagnostic X-ray." *Pediatrics* 28 (1961): 676.

The following articles are representative of the interdisciplinary investigation on radiation effects during early development. Members of the Departments of Anatomy, Pediatrics, Pathology, Radiology, Biophysics–Nuclear Medicine, and Brain Research Institute at the UCLA School of Medicine participated.

Billings, M. S., J. N. Yamazaki, L. R. Bennett, and B. G. Lamson. "Late Effects of Low-Dose Whole Body X-Irradiation on Four-Day-Old Rats." In *Radiation Effects in Physics, Chemistry, and Biology,* ed. H. Ebert and A. Howard, pp. 395–96. Proceedings of the Second International Congress of Radiation Research, Harrogate, England, August 5–11, 1962. Amsterdam: North Holland Publishing, 1963.

Clemente, C. C., J. N. Yamazaki, L. R. Bennett, R. McFall, and E. H. Maynard. "The Effects of Ionizing X-Irradiation on the Adult and Immature Brain." In *Proceedings of the Second United Nations International Conference on the Peaceful Uses of Atomic Energy,* pp. 282–86. Geneva: United Nations Publication 22, 1956.

Mosier, H. D., Jr., and R. A. Janson. "Stunted Growth in Rats Following X-Irradiation of the Head." *Growth* 31 (1967): 139–48.

Schjeide, O. A., K. Haack, J. de Vellis, J. N. Yamazaki, and C. D. Clemente. "Radiation Effects of Myelination Radiation Research." Abstract for the 14th Annual Meeting of the Radiation Research Society, Coronado, Calif., February 13–16, 1966.

Schjeide, O. A., J. N. Yamazaki, and C. D. Clemente. "Biochemical Effects of Irradiation in the Brain of the Neonatal Rat." In *Response of the Nervous System to Ionizing Radiation,* ed. T. J. Hayley and R. S. Snyder, pp. 95–109. New York: Academic Press, 1962.

Yamazaki, J. N., L. Bennett, and C. D. Clemente. "Behavioral and Histological Effects of Head X-Irradiation in Newborn Rats." In *Response of the Nervous System to Ionizing Radiation*, ed. T. J. Hayley and R. S. Snyder, pp. 59–74. New York: Academic Press, 1962.

12   Emerging Answers

Blot, W. J., and R. W. Miller. "Mental Retardation Following in Utero Exposure to the Atomic Bomb." *Radiology* 106 (1973): 617.

Boice, John D., and Joseph F. Fraumeni, eds. *Radiation Carcinogenesis — Epidemiology and Biological Significance*. Progress in Cancer Research and Therapy 26. New York: Raven Press, 1984.

Burrow, Gerald N., Delbert A. Fisher, and P. Reed Larsen. "Maternal and Fetal Thyroid Function." *New England Journal of Medicine* 331 (1994): 1072–78.

Cao, X. Y., X. M. Jiang, et al. "Timing of Vulnerability of the Brain to Iodine Deficiency in Endemic Cretinism." *New England Journal of Medicine* 331 (1994): 1739–44.

Conard, Robert. "Fallout: The Experiences of a Medical Team in the Care of Marshallese Population Accidentally Exposed to Fallout Radiation." Brookhaven National Laboratory Report, BNL 46444. Medical Department, Brookhaven National Laboratory Associated University, Inc. Upton, N.Y.: U.S. Department of Energy, 1992.

Conard, R. A., and A. Hicking. "Medical Findings in Marshallese People Exposed to Fallout Radiation." *Journal of the American Medical Association* 192 (1965): 457.

Conard, R. A., E. E. Paglia, P. R. Larsen, W. W. Sutow, B. M. Dobyns, J. Robbins, W. A. Krotsky, J. K. Cong, J. S. Robinson, and W. L. Milne. "Review of Medical Findings in a Marshallese Population Twenty-six Years after Accidental Exposure to Radioactive Fallout." Brookhaven National Laboratory Report, BNL 51261. Springfield, Va.: National Technical Information Service, 1980.

Conference on Pediatric Significance of Peacetime Radioactive Fallout. Sponsored by American Academy of Pediatrics in conjunction with U.S. Public Health Service and the Atomic Energy Commission. J. Yamazaki, Co-chairman of the session "Radioactivity in the Individual," San Diego, March 14–16, 1966. *Pediatrics* 4, no. 1, pt. 3, suppl. (January 1968).

Cronkite, E. P., V. P. Bond, and C. L. Dunham, eds. *Some Effects of Ionizing Radiation on Human Beings. A Report of the Marshallese and Americans Accidentally Exposed to Radiation from Fallout and a Discussion of Radiation Injury in Human*

Beings. U.S. Atomic Energy Commission. AEC-TID 5385. Washington, D.C.: U.S. Government Printing Office, 1956.

Effects of Radiation and Other Deleterious Agents on Embryonic Development. Symposium of the Research Conference for Biology and Medicine of the Atomic Energy Commission, sponsored by the Biology Division, Oak Ridge National Laboratory, Oak Ridge, Tenn., April 20–23, 1953. *Journal of Cellular and Comparative Physiology* 43, suppl. 1 (1954).

Eisenbud, M. "The *Lucky Dragon (Fukuryu Maru)* Incident and ABCC." *RERF Update,* vol. 5, pt. 1, p. 10 (Spring 1993); pt. 2, p. 8 (Summer 1993).

Fisher, D. A., and B. L. Foley. "Early Treatment of Congenital Hypothyroidism." *Pediatrics* 83 (1989): 785–89.

Folley, J. H., W. Borges, and T. Yamawaki. "Incidence of Leukemia in Survivors of the Atomic Bomb in Hiroshima and Nagasaki." *American Journal of Medicine* 131 (1952): 311–21.

Hetzel, B. S. Editorial: "Iodine and Fetal Brain Damage." *New England Journal of Medicine,* 311 (1994): 170–71.

Ichimaru, M., T. Ohkita, and T. Ishimaru. "Leukemia, Multiple Myeloma, and Malignant Lymphoma." In *Cancer in Atomic Bomb Survivors,* ed. I. Shigematsu and A. Kagan. Gann Monograph on Cancer Research no. 32. Tokyo: Japan Scientific Societies Press; New York: Plenum Press, 1986.

Lapp, Ralph E. *The Voyage of the Lucky Dragon.* New York: Harper and Brothers, 1957.

Mabuchi, K., M. Soda, E. Ron, M. Tokunaga, S. Ochikubo, S. Sugimoto, T. Ikeda, M. Terasaki, R. L. Preston, and D. E. Thompson. "Cancer Incidence in Atomic Bomb Survivors. Part 1: Use of Tumor Registries in Hiroshima and Nagasaki for Incidence Studies." RERF Special Report 1994. *Radiation Research* 137 (1994): S1–S16.

March, H. C. "Leukemia in Radiologists." *Radiology* 43 (1944): 275.

Martland, H. S. "The Occurrence of Malignancy in Radioactive Persons (Luminous-Radium Dial Painters)." *American Journal of Cancer* 15 (1931): 24–35.

Miller, R. W. "Delayed Effects Occurring within the First Decade after Exposure of Young Individuals to the Hiroshima Atomic Bomb." *Pediatrics* 18 (1956): 1–18.

Miller, R. W., and W. J. Blot. "Small Head Size after Exposure to the Atomic Bomb." *Lancet* (1972): 784.

Otake, M., H. Yoshimaru, and W. J. Schull. "Severe Mental Retardation among Prenatally Exposed Survivors of the Atomic Bombing of Hiroshima and Nagasaki.

A Comparison of the T65DR and DS86 Dosimetry Systems." Technical Report, Radiation Effects Research Foundation, 1987, pp. 16–87.

Plummer, G. "Anomalies Occurring in Children Exposed in Utero to the Atomic Bomb in Hiroshima." *Pediatrics* 10 (1953): 687.

Preston, D. L., S. Kusumi, M. Tomonaga, S. Izumi, E. Ron, A. Kuramoto, N. Kamada, H. Dohy, T. Matsui, H. Nonaka, D. E. Thompson, M. Soda, and K. Mabuchi. "Part III: Leukemia, Lymphoma, and Multiple Myeloma, 1950–1987." RERF Special Report 1994. *Radiation Research* 137 (1994): S68–S97.

"Review of Forty-five Year Study of Hiroshima and Nagasaki Atomic Bomb Survivors." Japan Radiation Research Society, Chiba, Japan. *Journal of Radiation Research* 32, suppl. (1991).

"Review of Thirty Year Study of Hiroshima and Nagasaki Atomic Bomb Survivors." Japan Radiation Research Society, Chiba, Japan. *Journal of Radiation Research* 16, suppl. no. 16 (1975).

Ron, E., D. L. Preston, K. Mabuchi, D. E. Thompson, and M. Soda. "Part IV: Comparison of Cancer Incidence and Mortality." RERF Special Report 1994. *Radiation Research* 137 (1994): S98–S112.

Shigematsu, Itsuzo, and Abraham Kagan, eds. *Cancer in Atomic Bomb Survivors.* Gann Monograph on Cancer Research no. 32. Tokyo: Japan Scientific Societies Press; New York: Plenum Press, 1986.

Shimizu, Y., H. Kato, and W. Schull. "Studies of the Mortality of A-Bomb Survivors. Mortality, 1950–1985. Part 2: Cancer Mortality on Recently Revised Doses *(DS86)."* *Radiation Research* 121 (1990): 120–41 [RERF TR 5-88].

Sutow, W. W., R. A. Conard, and K. M. Griffith. "Growth Status of Children Exposed to Fallout Radiation on Marshall Islands." *Pediatrics* 36 (1965): 72.

Tabuchi, M., T. Hirai, et al. "Clinical Findings on in Utero Exposed Microcephalic Children." *Atomic Bomb Casualty Commission Technical Report* 28 (1967): 67.

Tajima, E. "Dawn of Radiation Effects Research." *RERF Update*, vol. 5, pt. 3 (Autumn 1993). [Describes the *Fukuryu* incident and the social, political, and scientific consequences. The global implication resulted in establishment of the United Nations Scientific Committee on the Effects of Atomic Radiation in 1955, of which the author, Tajima, was appointed secretary.]

Thompson, Donovan J., ed. *U.S.-Japan Joint Workshop for Reassessment of Atomic Bomb Radiation Dosimetry in Hiroshima and Nagasaki.* Proceedings of workshop held in Nagasaki, Japan, February 16–17, 1983. Hiroshima: Radiation Effects Research Foundation, 1983.

Thompson, D. E., K. Mabuchi, E. Ron, M. Soda, M. Tokunaga, S. Ochikubo, S. Sugimoto, T. Ikeda, S. Izumi, M. Terasaki, and D. L. Preston. "Part II: Solid Tumors,
1958–1987." RERF Special Report 1994. *Radiation Research* 137 (1994): S17–S67.

Yamazaki, J. N. "A Review of the Literature of the Radiation Dosage Required to
Cause Manifest Central Nervous System Disturbance from in Utero and Postnatal
Exposure." *Pediatrics* 36, no. 5, pt. 2, suppl. (May 1966).

Yamazaki, J. N., and W. J. Schull. "Perinatal Loss and Neurological Abnormalities
among Children of the Atomic Bomb: Nagasaki and Hiroshima Revisited, 1949–
1989." *Journal of the American Medical Association* 264 (1990): 605–9.

Yamazaki, J. N., S. W. Wright, and P. Wright. "A Study of the Outcome of Pregnancy
in Women Exposed to the Atomic Bomb in Nagasaki." A.M.A. *American Journal
of Diseases of Children* 87 (1954): 448–63. [With a fuller discussion including
the outcome of pregnancy in World War II during the siege of Leningrad, in
Budapest, and in Holland.]

14 Farewell in Hiroshima

Dower, John W., and John Jukerman, eds. *The Hiroshima Murals: The Art of Iri
Maruki and Toshi Maruki.* Tokyo: Kodansha International, 1985. [The Marukis
arrived in Hiroshima a few days after the atomic bomb was dropped, tending the
injured, building shelters, searching for food, and cremating the dead.]

Field, Norma. *In the Realm of a Dying Emperor: Japan at Century's End.* New
York: Vintage Books, 1991. [See chapter 3, "Nagasaki — The Mayor" (Motoshima
Hitoshi).]

Institute of Medicine, National Academy of Sciences. *The Medical Implications of
Nuclear War,* ed. Frederic Solomon and Robert W. Marstion. Washington, D.C.:
National Academy Press, 1986.

Iri, Toshi. *Hiroshima no Pica.* Tokyo: Komine Shoten; New York: Lothrop, Lee and
Shepard, 1980. [A picture book for very young readers.]

Lifton, Robert J. *Death in Life: Survivors of Hiroshima.* New York: Simon and Schuster, 1967.

Maruki, Iri, and Toshi Maruki. *The Hiroshima Panels — Genbaku no Zu Maruki.*
Gallery for the Hiroshima Foundation. Saitama: Higashi-matsuyama, 1972. [In
1989, before returning to the United States, I spent an afternoon with the Marukis at their gallery in rural Saitama and viewed their murals, which revealed
what words alone cannot express — their sense of the tragedy of war to humanity.]

Nuclear Enchantment. Photographs by Patrick Nagatani, essay by Eugenia Parry Janis. Albuquerque: University of New Mexico Press, 1991. [A photographic tableau reflecting the future nuclear era, with its fear and environmental contamination depicted in the background of the desert pueblo country of New Mexico, birthplace of the atomic bomb.]

Office of Technology Assessment. *The Effects of Nuclear War.* Washington, D.C.: U.S. Government Printing Office, 1979. [OTA provides Congress with independent and timely information about the potential effects, both beneficial and harmful, of technical applications.]

Omuta, Minoru. "The Microcephalic Children of Hiroshima." *Japan Quarterly* 8, no. 3 (1966): 375–84.

Oughterson, Ashley, and Warren Shields. "Mortality of Shielded and Unshielded Students in Relation to Distance in Hiroshima." In *Medical Effects of the Atomic Bomb in Japan,* p. 35. National Nuclear Energy Series, Manhattan Project, Technical Section Division VIII, vol. 8. New York: McGraw-Hill, 1956.

Sakaguchi, Tayori, and Shinichiro Murakami. *Nagasaki Bomb Series Pika Don (Lightning Flash) and Children,* 6 vols. [*Nagasaki Bakudan-Pica-Don to Kodomotachi*]. Kokura: Araki Shoten, 1980. [This graded illustrated series is used as teaching manuals for peace for grade-school students. Mr. Sakaguchi is a survivor of the bombing in Nagasaki. Mr. Murakami, the illustrator and a native of Nagasaki, was in the armed forces at the time of the bombing but knew many children who perished in the aftermath of the explosion.]

Tsuzuki, Masao. *Medical Report on Atomic Bomb Effects.* Medical Section, Special Committee for the Effects of the Atomic Bomb, National Research Council of Japan, January 1947 (translated into English in 1953).

Biographical Note

Born in 1916 in Los Angeles, James N. Yamazaki attended the University of California at Los Angeles and Marquette University Medical School. He was a battalion surgeon with the 106th Infantry Division in the Battle of the Bulge and witnessed American aerial bombing in Germany as a prisoner of war. He was the first Physician In Charge of the Nagasaki Atomic Bomb Casualty Commission from 1949 to 1951. He is a Clinical Professor of Pediatrics at the University of California at Los Angeles, where he initiated an interdisciplinary investigation of the medical and biological effects of radiation on unborn and young children.

Louis B. Fleming, a retired journalist, is now active in community and church volunteer work in Pasadena. He was born in Pittsburgh on April 16, 1925, and is a graduate of the Polytechnic School in Pasadena, the Webb School in Claremont, and Stanford University. He was in the U.S. Navy in World War II and served as an officer in Japan during the American occupation in 1946. He has been a friend of Dr. Yamazaki and his family since childhood. During the last thirty years of his career before retirement in 1990 he worked for the *Los Angeles Times* as a staff writer, foreign correspondent, editorial writer, and chief editorial writer. As a *Times* correspondent Mr. Fleming accompanied Pope John Paul II on his historic visits to Hiroshima and Nagasaki.

Library of Congress Cataloging-in-Publication Data

Yamazaki, James N.

Children of the atomic bomb : an American physician's memoir of
Nagasaki, Hiroshima, and the Marshall islands / James N. Yamazaki
with Louis B. Fleming.

p. cm. — (Asia-Pacific: Culture, Politics, and Society)

Includes bibliographical references and index.

ISBN 0-8223-1658-7 (alk. paper).

1. Yamazaki, James N.   2. Pediatricians — United States — Biography.

3. Atomic bomb victims — Medical care — Japan — Hiroshima-shi.

4. Atomic bomb victims — Medical care — Japan — Nagasaki-shi.

5. Atomic bomb victims — Medical care — Marshall Islands.

I. Fleming, Louis B.   II. Title.   III. Series.

RJ43.Y36A3   1995

618.92'9897'0092 — dc20   95-6683   CIP

[B]